GW00671531

British Housewives' message to YOU!

"MAKE YOUR *FOOD* GO FURTHER WITH WEETABIX"

Here is a way to save a meal-a-week.

Weetabix Cheese Savoury

4 Weetabix. Seasoning
½ pint white sauce.
Grated cheese to taste.

Remains of cooked cauliflower or other cooked vegetables. Cut a little off the top of each Weetabix, or slice in half. Heat through under grill. Mix the cooked vegetables with sufficient sauce to moisten, add seasoning and grated cheese to flavour. Pile with vegetable mixture on the Weetabix, sprinkle thickly with Weetabix crumbs and grated cheese, and brown under the grill. Serve at once in a hot dish. Any remaining sauce can be poured round. Not only a most delicious savoury for four people, but really a meal in itself.

More Weetabix is being made. If at times it is difficult to obtain this is because more people are buying it.

Standard Size 7½d.
Double Size 1/1d.

WEETABIX LTD., WEETABIX MILLS, BURTON LATIMER, NORTHANTS

For putting rich beefiness into soups, stews, and gravies there's nothing like OXO. It makes meals meatier and appetites healthier.

GOOD FARE

A BOOK OF WARTIME
RECIPES

COMPILED BY

The Daily Telegraph HOME COOK

This edition first published by Macmillan 2008
an imprint of Pan Macmillan Ltd
Pan Macmillan, 20 New Wharf Road, London NI 9RR
Basingstoke and Oxford
Associated companies throughout the world
www.panmacmillan.com

ISBN 978-0-230-71025-2

1 3 5 7 9 8 6 4 2

A CIP catalogue record for this book is available from
the British Library.

Printed and bound in the UK by
CPI Mackays, Chatham ME5 8TD

CONTENTS

PART I

THE NEW COOKERY

PART II

STOCKING THE STORE CUPBOARD

FOREWORD

NEW times necessitate new cookery. The old cookery books have become out of date for application to the tables, larders and store-cupboards of a changing world.

This is a compilation of practical recipes, research results and hints which make for economic marketing, catering and cooking, by *The Daily Telegraph* Home Cook. Housewives have sought her guidance in the satisfactory solution of new problems in housekeeping, and their enquiries have revealed what women in general were wanting to know about the new catering and cooking in order that they might rule out waste of food, fuel and time and yet feed their families well.

The comprehensive collection of recipes now brought together in volume form is built up on realities and not on theories. True economy in the kitchen does not mean monotonous, dull, unattractive fare but entirely the opposite. The housewife of this generation is called on as never before to keep members of her household healthy, efficient and happy. Good food is essential, food that stimulates, nourishes and pleases and the key to Good Fare is variety.

The recipes show how to use the bountiful supplies of home-grown provender, particularly vegetables, from day to day and for stocking the store-cupboards ; how to meet the requirements of unconventional mealtimes that have in many cases taken the place of the old rota of four meals a day. There are many suggestions for main dishes of the day, for the use of butcher's "sundries" and for, homely teatime delicacies. In recipes requiring some flavouring or other ingredient that may be difficult to get, a point is made of suggesting an alternative. Regional cookery has been drawn on and brought into modern practice by careful adaptation. There can be no better basis of cookery than that provided by generations of housewives who have brought homely fare to epicurean perfection. Use of time-saving canned foods and other preserved products, of the excellent margarine at our disposal and the art of flavouring which is one of the great secrets of economy in the preparation of food are other subjects featured.

Readers' own recipes provide a special section devoted largely to their highly developed art of making the most of ingredients at their disposal. Canteen recipes that meet a wide range of tastes, home as well as institutional, form another distinctive section. These recipes can be scaled down to the requirements of the small home kitchen. Equally so, they furnish a guide for those called on to deal with community feeding.

Simple but Better Fare is the aim of the New Cookery

PART I

CHAPTER I

SOUP BOWL ECONOMY

QUICKLY prepared soups to fill the soup bowls and covered cups that are now preferred to shallow plates are in request. The old stock-pot essential to the making of so many of the classic soups and the prolonged cooking required have to be ruled out and a new technique followed.

Liquid in which vegetables such as potatoes, carrots, turnips, celery, green peas, leeks and so on have been boiled is the basis of many good soups, thick and thin. One vegetable is selected to give predominant flavour ; tomatoes, cauliflowers, onions, carrots, green peas are excellent used in this way. Cereals, rice, barley, oatmeal, cornflour, give thickness. Shredded lettuce or cabbage, chopped watercress or sorrel gathered from the fields are suitable additions in some cases. A little margarine or clarified dripping in which vegetables may be fried lightly adds to the flavour and milk, when available, can be used with vegetable stock. Other ingredients are herbs, fresh from the garden or dried from the store cupboard, nutmeg and mace among spices, and pepper and salt as required.

For a brown soup the vegetables are well fried, and meat extract or cubes may be added. Grated cheese may be served separately with any soup. This is a good way of using up stale cheese and improves food value.

9

CAULIFLOWER CREAM

1 small white cauliflower.	2 ozs. margarine.
1 teaspoonful chopped onion.	1 quart water or water and milk.
1 level tablespoonful cornflour.	Pepper and salt, grate of nutmeg.

Break cauliflower into small sprays. Boil with onion in water to which a little salt has been added. Drain, rub through sieve, return to pan containing liquid in which cauliflower was cooked. Add margarine, seasoning and nutmeg, simmer for 15 minutes, thicken with cornflour, mixed to a paste with a little stock.

LENTIL OR SPLIT PEA SOUP

½ pint lentils or split peas.	Bouquet garni (thyme, parsley, bayleaf tied together) or dried herbs, dried or chopped mint
1 onion, 1 carrot, 1 small turnip.	
½ cupful celery cut in small pieces.	2 pints water.
1 oz. dripping or margarine.	½ pint milk.
	Seasoning.

Soak lentils or peas overnight. Slice vegetables, place in saucepan with lentils, water, herbs and seasoning. Simmer 1½ to 2 hours, stir occasionally. Rub through sieve, keeping back a few pieces of carrot. Reheat soup with milk, stirring in fat. Serve in individual cups with pieces of carrot floating in each cup and mint sprinkled over.

TOMATO SOUP

½ teacupful tomato puree.	1 tablespoonful rice.
1 pint veal stock or water.	Salt and pepper.
1 carrot.	

Put stock in saucepan. Season, add rice, grated carrot,

tomato puree, and after bringing to boil simmer for 20 minutes or longer.

Chopped watercress with a little margarine, green peas, cauliflower or any other vegetable could take the place of tomato puree. Addition of a little milk is an improvement.

VEGETABLE SOUP

1 pint shelled green peas.	2 ozs. margarine.
2 lettuces shredded.	2 tablespoonfuls bread
A few spinach leaves.	crumbs.
1 teaspoonful chopped onion.	Pepper and salt to taste.
½ teaspoonful sugar.	1 quart water or light vegetable stock.

Cook peas with onion, lettuces, and margarine in half the quantity of liquid. When peas are soft, sieve, adding at same time the spinach leaves which have been cooked separately. Their purpose is to make the soup a brighter green in colour, but they are an optional ingredient. Restore all to pan with remainder of liquid, bread-crumbs, seasoning and sugar. Heat thoroughly. A few whole green peas or a teaspoonful of chopped mint may be added before serving.

WATERCRESS CREAM

1 lb. watercress.	1½ pints water or water
½ lb. mashed potatoes	and milk.
2 ozs. margarine.	Seasoning to taste.

Chop watercress and cook gently in saucepan with margarine. Add mashed potatoes, stirring all the time, and then, gradually, the liquid. Simmer for a few minutes, pass through a hair sieve, season. Heat up. The addition of the yolk of an egg in final reheating is an improvement.

WINTER SOUP

1 lb. carrots.	2 tablespoonfuls cooked
3 pints water or stock.	rice.
1 onion, 1 leek, stick of celery.	A pinch each of nutmeg, salt, sugar and mixed
2 ozs. dripping.	herbs, salt and pepper.
Few bacon rinds.	

Prepare vegetables by cutting them into small pieces. Melt dripping in saucepan, put in all the vegetables and bacon rinds. Put on lid and cook gently for a few minutes, shaking the pan to prevent burning. Then add stock or water, mixed herbs, salt and pepper. Continue simmering gently till vegetables are soft and pulpy. Rub through a sieve and add a pinch of sugar and nutmeg. Return to saucepan to reheat, adding the rice well cooked and dry.

CHAPTER II

CHEAPER FISH MADE INTERESTING

CUT-AND-DRIED plans must have no place in the catering scheme when the housewife goes to the fishmonger. Often it is advisable to try out the less familiar and cheaper kinds of fish, bearing in mind that the most expensive are not necessarily the best.

Home cooks have been content to ring the changes on cod, hake, halibut, fresh haddock, mackerel and herrings among fresh fish, and smoked haddock, kippers and bloaters. These are all good fish, but there are others that might well make more frequent appearance on the family table.

Fish new to the ordinary British market have come along recently. "Government" fresh salted cod, and

smoked, fresh cod, open out new problems in the culinary art to the intelligent cook with a bent for research. Both lend themselves to such dishes as creamed fish, pies or cakes, and the popular and economical kedgeree.

The use of a greater variety of vegetables with fish is another direction in which research is well worth while. In the higher branches of fish cookery much is done with mushrooms, artichoke hearts, asparagus points and the universally popular tomatoes. Home cooks might seek triumphs by way of carrots, parsnips, beetroots, Jerusalem artichokes, spinach and with herbs other than parsley.

Cereals, rice and oatmeal are advised ; grated cheese, forcemeats, are other suggestions. Herrings and mackerel may be sprinkled with oatmeal before frying or grilling.

BAKED BREAM

This inexpensive fish, although suitable as main luncheon dish with plain boiled, mashed or fried potatoes, is somewhat overlooked.

1 bream between 1½ and 2 lbs.	Margarine or dripping for baking.
White sauce, flavouring, seasoning.	

Do not remove scales but fish should be well washed and carefully cleaned. Dry and bake in hot fat till tender but firm. Baste and turn in cooking, which will require about 25 minutes in moderate oven. Scales and skin are removed before fish goes to table. Serve with white sauce flavoured with tomato, anchovy, parsley or mixed herbs

BLOATER FRITTERS

2 bloaters.	Pepper and salt to taste
1 tablespoonful grated cheese.	Frying batter.

Go carefully with salt, as bloaters are often salty. Remove

head and skin, split and bone, make into neat fillets. Add cheese and seasoning to frying batter ; dip fillets in and fry till golden brown and crisp.

This inexpensive little dish is suitable for breakfast, supper, luncheon or as a substantial snack.

CALCUTTA CURRY

1 lb. any white fish.	1 teaspoonful flour.
½ pint milk or fish stock.	1 dessertspoonful curry powder.
1 onion.	
2 chopped chillies.	1 teaspoonful curry paste.
1 oz. dripping.	Salt.

Melt dripping in saucepan, fry onion till lightly brown (keeping back a few slices to sprinkle over curry when serving), add chopped chillies, curry powder and paste. Cook a few minutes. Add flour, mix thoroughly, add milk or stock and salt to taste. Simmer 15 minutes. Add the fish previously boiled and flaked, or fried (in latter case do not flake). Cook a few minutes to heat thoroughly. Garnish with fried onion. Serve with boiled rice and chutney.

COD'S ROE CASSEROLE

1½ lbs. cod's roe.	Pepper and salt.
½ lb. fat bacon.	

Boil the roe for 20 minutes, allow to cool. Peel and cut into rounds about ½ inch thick. Cut bacon into strips, having removed rind. Line a greased casserole with the bacon, continue to fill it with alternate layers of cod's roe and bacon, seasoning each layer, and finishing with bacon. Bake in moderate oven ¾ hour.

This dish is delicious either hot or cold. Parsley sauce should be served if hot.

FISH CHOWDER

¾ lb. fish (whiting, cod, plaice or haddock).
4 potatoes.
3 or 4 slices chopped fat bacon or pickled pork.
1 finely sliced onion.
Pinch of dried herbs.

2 teaspoonfuls chopped parsley.
2 or 3 chopped mushrooms (optional).
½ pint water.
Seasoning.

For Sauce

½ gill breadcrumbs.
¼ pint milk.

½ oz. margarine.
½ oz. flour.

Wash fish, cut into small pieces. Place fish, potatoes and bacon in alternate layers in saucepan with sliced onion, mushrooms and herbs between the layers, also pepper and salt. Add water, cook with lid on 30 to 40 minutes.

Make white sauce with flour, margarine and milk, add breadcrumbs to it, and when boiling add to fish and potatoes. Cook another 10 minutes.

MUSSELS WITH SAUCE

1 quart of mussels.

For Sauce

1½ tablespoonfuls vinegar.
1½ tablespoonfuls stock or water.
1 level dessertspoonful cornflour or plain flour.

1 teaspoonful chopped parsley.
1 shallot or 1 teaspoonful onion finely chopped.
Seasoning.

Mussels should be washed carefully and allowed to cook in covered pan in a small quantity of water to which a few drops of the vinegar have been added. Remove shells and "beards" after about 10 minutes. Keep hot and pour sauce over made by boiling together the vinegar, shallot or onion, parsley and seasoning and thickening with cornflour made to a paste with stock or water. Reserve a little of the parsley to sprinkle over top of mussels.

PIQUANT FISH MAYONNAISE

1½ lbs. any cold fish (salmon, turbot, cod, fresh haddock, plaice, sole, rock salmon or whiting).

Lettuce or endive.

Tomato, cucumber, beetroot.

A few slices of anchovy, gherkins, capers, mayonnaise. (*See* under "Sauces and Salad Dressings".)

Remove skin and bones from fish, break into flakes. Pile fish on bed of lettuce or endive leaves. Pour over it a piquant mayonnaise. This is made by adding a little chopped gherkin and capers to the mayonnaise. Garnish with tomato, beetroot, cucumber and thin fillets of anchovy.

SOUSED MACKEREL, HERRINGS OR PILCHARDS

2 or 3 mackerel or 4 or 5 herrings or pilchards.

Salt, pepper.

3 cloves.

10 peppercorns.

1 bay leaf, pinch mace.

Vinegar.

Finely sliced onion (optional).

Wash fish, remove heads and tails, fillet and remove bones. Place in layers with roes in a pie dish or casserole with onion, spices and flavourings sprinkled between. Cover with vinegar or vinegar and water. Bake in moderate oven about 1 hour.

STUFFED HADDOCK

1 fresh haddock.

For Forcemeat

4 ozs. breadcrumbs.

2 tablespoonfuls chopped suet or melted margarine.

½ teaspoonful mixed herbs, pinch of mace.

1 teaspoonful anchovy sauce.

Pepper, salt.

1 egg or about 6 tablespoonfuls milk to bind.

Wash, clean and scrape fish. Make forcemeat, keeping back a few breadcrumbs and a little margarine, stuff fish with it, and tie or sew up opening. Put in a well-greased baking tin or glass ovenware dish. Cover with breadcrumbs and pats of margarine. Bake in moderate oven 40 minutes.

WHITE FISH CREAMS

1 lb. uncooked white fish.	2 ozs. margarine.
4 ozs. breadcrumbs.	1 teaspoonful finely chopped parsley.
½ teaspoonful anchovy essence (optional)	
1 egg.	Salt, pepper, pinch of nutmeg
¼ pint milk	

Remove skin and bones from fish, cut into small pieces. Mix fish, breadcrumbs, anchovy essence, beaten egg, parsley, nutmeg, seasoning and, lastly, melted margarine with milk. Stir all ingredients well together. Turn into greased moulds. Cover with greased paper and steam 1½ hours. The creams can alternatively be baked in a moderate oven for 45 minutes.

Serve with caper or white sauce.

CHAPTER III

IN PLACE OF THE ROAST

ROASTING is a branch of cookery in which British cooks excel. The roast sirloin with its horseradish, saddle of mutton and red-currant jelly, and roast lamb accompanied by mint sauce, can stand for perfection, but never for economy. Too much of their goodness is diffused in the inviting aroma they give forth while cooking. The modern trend, from choice no less than necessity, is all for small joints, and these do not always lend themselves to roasting. Some suggestions other than roasts are given here.

In the section that deals with homely dishes of the day, the housewife will find the indispensable hotpot, the stew, boiled meats with their respective vegetables and other dishes that are the standby of the restaurant as of the home kitchen.

Other pages tell the cook the best ways of serving what is known in the meat trade as "offal". Butchers' "sundries" is a pleasanter kitchen term for liver, kidney, heart, ox-tail, sweetbreads, cowheel, calf's foot, pig's trotter, tripe and other items that yield so many savoury, inexpensive dishes.

Last but not least is pie-making, which has flourished in our land for centuries. There are favourite pies that come down to us with an Elizabethan call. Chicken and mutton pies, subject of street calls in the days of the Tudors, for example ; the pies of nursery song, blackbird and partridge ; country pies with the classic Melton Mowbray leading ; Royal pies like the Windsor. Many of the old pies have survived in the home, but the recipes have changed from decade to decade to meet new tastes.

Pies help the cook to feed her family well, especially now when so many vegetables form part of the ingredients.

Potatoes, tomatoes, mushrooms, when reasonably priced, apples, onions, carrots are all used freely. Force-meat balls (breadcrumbs, suet or margarine, herbs and seasoning) and a covering of pastry contribute to an economical dish for main meal of the day.

BREAST OF VEAL

(For Small Family)

This shows what can be done with 1¼ lbs. breast of veal. Cut up flap, separate meat from gristle and bone.

Place everything in bowl with a little salt, few drops vinegar, cover with boiling water to blanch. Pour water away after 3 minutes and place contents of bowl in saucepan with cold water to cover. Simmer gently till flesh is tender ; do not season yet. This makes two main dishes with stock left over for soup. (*See* under "Soups.")

(1) *Casserole :*

Veal from flap.	Pepper, salt and thyme.
1 teaspoonful chopped onion.	1 oz. margarine.
	1 dessertspoonful flour.
1 tablespoonful chopped or grated carrot.	Veal stock, parsley.

Place pieces of veal in a casserole with the onion, carrot, seasoning to taste, and sufficient veal stock to cover. Simmer gently. Make sauce by adding flour, cooked for a few minutes in margarine melted in a saucepan. Pour over, garnish dish with chopped parsley.

(2) *Pie :*

Remainder of veal.	Veal stock, seasoning, pastry.
2 rashers bacon.	
Small forcemeat balls.	

Cut up bacon and veal and arrange in shallow pie dish. Season to taste. Fill up dish with forcemeat balls. Add some of the liquid in which veal was cooked, and cover dish with pastry. Bake till pale golden brown.

BRISKET OR FLANK OF BEEF

About 2½ lbs. brisket or flank of beef.	1 teaspoonful spiced vinegar (vinegar from pickled walnuts is good).
1 oz. dripping.	1 bayleaf.
1 teaspoonful brown sugar.	Salt and pepper

Brisket and flank of beef both need plenty of cooking. They may be done in a "pot roast" and the oven saved.

Trim joint, take out bone to facilitate carving, and brown both sides in dripping in saucepan. Put seasonings, sugar and vinegar on the meat. See that the bottom of the saucepan is covered with sufficient hot water to prevent burning.

Place lid on saucepan, bring to boil and cook slowly for 2½ hours. Baste with rich liquid yielded by the joint. Remove from heat but leave joint in its covered saucepan to cool gradually.

Serve cold with salad, a dish of beetroot or any pickle. Flavour and tenderness will come as a surprise to those who have not tasted these cheap cuts done by this method.

BROWN FRICASSEED RABBIT

1 rabbit.
2 ozs. dripping or margarine.
1 onion.

1 level tablespoonful flour.
Water, seasoning, herbs—sage is a good choice.

Have rabbit neatly jointed and fry with liver and heart in dripping or margarine with sliced onion till light brown. Work flour into fat in pan, add water to make enough gravy barely to cover rabbit, add seasoning and herbs. Simmer gently till rabbit is tender, about 1½ hours. A rasher of fat bacon cut into strips and fried with rabbit is good addition.

JUGGED HARE

1 hare.
2 carrots, 2 turnips, 1 stick celery, 1 onion.
1 rasher fat bacon.
2 tablespoonfuls flour.

1½ pints water.
Forcemeat, bouquet garni and seasoning, a little dripping.
Red-currant or rowan jelly.

This is one of the most savoury dishes known to cookery. The hare can be bought ready for jugging and jointed.

Fry the hare, neatly jointed, with cut-up vegetables, in dripping. Add flour to fat, stirring carefully to avoid lumps, then the water, herbs and seasoning. If liked the onion may be stuck with 1 or 2 cloves.

Simmer gently for 2 hours, adding small forcemeat balls ½ an hour before serving. Red-currant or rowan-berry jelly is served with jugged hare.

MANCHESTER STEAKS

½ lb. stewing steak or ¼ lb. each steak and kidney.	Pinch of mace, nutmeg and mixed herbs.
1 teaspoonful chopped parsley.	Batter for frying (milk and flour).
1 onion.	2 ozs. dripping.

Remove skin and gristle from meat and pass twice through mincer. Put into a basin with the onion finely chopped, parsley, spices and herbs. Form into round, flat cakes, sprinkle with flour, dip in a batter made by mixing a little flour and milk to the consistency of cream. Fry steaks in hot dripping till browned both sides. Drain well, serve on hot dish with brown or tomato sauce. These steaks can also be grilled.

RABBIT CURRY

1 rabbit.	1 dessertspoonful curry powder.
1 medium-sized onion sliced thinly.	1 teaspoonful flour.
1 cooking apple chopped.	1 tumblerful water.
1 stick of celery cut up small.	Dripping.

Cut jointed rabbit in small pieces and fry in a little dripping ; remove from pan. Fry vegetables and apple in same fat and when soft, add flour and curry powder, working all well together before pouring in water. Return rabbit to pan and continue to cook it in curry sauce for 1½ to 2 hours. Serve with boiled rice. (*See* page 24.)

TOO PRECIOUS TO WASTE!

Now, more than ever before, you must be *sure* of avoiding dishes that are 'failures'. McDougall reliability is vital in your cookery success. Always use McDougall's for your war-time recipes—and you will never have disasters !

Mc Dougall's

THE SELF-RAISING FLOUR THAT GIVES SURE RESULTS

Rice for Curry

Wash rice well in several waters, put into a saucepan of boiling salted water (2 teaspoonfuls salt to 1 quart water). Boil 12 to 15 minutes, or till grains feel soft when squeezed between fingers. Strain. Run cold water over rice to separate grains. Dry on rack of stove or in oven, stirring with fork to separate grains. Keep hot till required.

SCRAG INTO FILLET

The despised scrag of mutton can be filleted carefully, made into a neat, compact cut, and cooked as a joint. There is no waste this way and the meat will be as "tender as chicken".

Ask the butcher to fillet required amount of scrag and shape into joint. It can be served in the following ways :

ROAST, hot or cold, stuffed with a light forcemeat, of the kind used for veal.

BOILED, with young root vegetables and accompanied by parsley sauce.

BROWN RAGOUT. To make this, fry sliced vegetables slightly in dripping in saucepan. Cut fillets in small pieces, sprinkle with flour, add to pan, brown slightly, season, add stock or water to cover, bring to boil, stew slowly 1½ hours.

WHITE BLANQUETTE with creamy sauce. 1 lb. filleted scrag, a little cooking fat, ½ oz. flour, 1½ gills warm water, 1 onion, pepper, salt, bouquet garni. Cut scrag into small pieces. Melt fat in saucepan, add meat, let it cook a little without browning. Remove meat. Make sauce by adding flour to fat in pan, cook a minute or two without browning. Add warm water by degrees, stir till boiling. Season with pepper, salt and bouquet garni. Place meat in sauce, cover pan, cook slowly 1 hour. Then add sliced onion, cook another hour.

Homely Dishes of the Day

BEEF SKIRT AND KIDNEY PUDDING

¾ lb. beef skirt or leg of beef (more economical than steak and flavour is better).
¼ lb. ox kidney.
1 small onion.

1 dessertspoonful mushroom ketchup, or 2 or 3 mushrooms.
1 tablespoonful flour.
Salt, pepper.
Suet pastry.

Line a greased pudding basin with suet pastry rolled out to about ¼ inch thick. Mix flour, salt and pepper on a plate. Cut beef and kidney into narrow strips, dip in seasoned flour, place small piece of kidney on each piece of beef and roll up. Place rolls in basin with finely sliced onion. Pour in a little more than ¼ pint boiling water. Moisten edges, put on pastry lid, tie floured cloth over it, put into boiling water or steamer. Boil 3 to 3½ hours.

BOILED BEEF, CARROTS AND DUMPLINGS

Small piece of fresh or salted beef (silverside in latter case is preferred).
Carrots.

1 or 2 small onions.
Parsley, thyme, bayleaf.
Pepper, salt.

For Dumplings

¼ lb. self-raising flour.
1½ ozs. suet.

Pinch of salt, cold water.

Carrots can be chief vegetable of the meal. Put meat in saucepan with tepid water to cover, bring to boil, then add carrots and onions sliced, also herbs and seasoning.

To make dumplings, mix flour with finely chopped suet, pinch of salt and enough water to make a soft dough. Put into liquor, which must be boiling, ½ hour before serving.

This homely dish can be made most attractive if garnished with halved gherkins and small mounds of well-drained cabbage moulded in egg-cups, or with unbroken Brussels sprouts.

BOILED MUTTON, TURNIPS AND CAPER SAUCE

2 lbs. best end neck of mutton.   3 carrots.
6 small turnips.   1 onion.

For Sauce

1 tablespoonful capers chopped.   1 teaspoonful vinegar to ½ pint seasoned white sauce.

Leg of mutton is regarded as the best boiling joint for the large family, but neck of mutton is more adaptable as regards size. Trim the piece of meat, removing excess of fat. Boil slowly with prepared vegetables—turnips in halves or quarters, according to size, carrots halved lengthwise, onion quartered or sliced—in salted water till tender.

Vegetables may be mashed or served whole, caper sauce separately in sauceboat. Parsley finely chopped may be substituted for capers. Stock provides excellent basis for soup for another meal.

BOILED PORK, PARSNIPS AND PEASE PUDDING

Pickled pork.   Pease pudding. (*See* under "Savoury Puddings".)
Parsnips as required.

This is an excellent cold-weather dish. Put pork into cold water, bring slowly to boil. Simmer gently—all pork should be well cooked, allow 25 minutes to each lb. Serve with plain boiled parsnips, whole or halved ; they should be added to pan 30 minutes before meat is cooked.

Parsley sauce goes well with this simple dish. Serve pease pudding with it.

LANCASHIRE HOT-POT

1½ lbs. scrag of mutton.
2 sheep's kidneys or ½ lb. ox kidney.
2 lbs. potatoes.
1 onion.
4 mushrooms or a little mushroom ketchup.

1 oz. margarine or dripping.
1 oz. flour.
¾ pint water.
Seasoning, parsley.

Melt dripping in pan, fry meat cut in small pieces and onion thinly sliced till brown. Remove from pan and add flour to fat, cook till brown, gradually add the water (hot) and mix well. Season.

Grease a casserole and put in layers the meat, onion and sliced kidney, and mushrooms cut in small pieces. Cover with potatoes thickly sliced. Pour over the browned gravy. Put on the lid and cook in moderate oven 2 hours. Half an hour before serving remove lid to brown potatoes. Sprinkle with finely chopped parsley and serve in casserole.

LIVER AND BACON

¾ lb. liver.
2 rashers fat bacon.
1 small sliced onion.
3 ozs. breadcrumbs.
1 dessertspoonful chopped parsley.

Pinch mixed herbs.
A little mushroom ketchup or Worcester sauce.
½ pint stock or water.
Seasoning.

Wash and dry liver, cut into slices and lay them in a greased casserole or pie dish. Mix onion, breadcrumbs, parsley, mixed herbs, pepper and salt. Sprinkle over the slices of liver, cover with strips of bacon. Pour stock or water and ketchup or sauce over liver. Cook in moderate oven ¾–1 hour.

SHEPHERD'S PIE

8 ozs. minced meat.	½ oz. dripping.
1 lb. mashed potatoes.	½ oz. flour.
1 onion sliced.	3 or 4 tablespoonfuls gravy
1 dessertspoonful Worcester sauce or mushroom ketchup.	—this can be made from meat extract.

Melt dripping in pan, fry finely sliced onion, add flour, cook a few minutes, add gravy. Grease pie dish, put in minced meat, pour in thickened gravy and mix well, season to taste. Pile mashed potatoes on top, put a few pats of margarine on the potatoes and bake in a good oven for 20 minutes.

STEWED TRIPE AND ONIONS

1 lb. tripe.	1 tablespoonful flour.
2 onions.	Pepper, salt.
½ oz. margarine.	

Put tripe into cold water and bring to boil. Strain, cut into oblong pieces about 2 inches long. Replace tripe in saucepan with sliced onions, seasoning, and stock from first boiling, with milk added to make enough liquid to cover. Simmer very gently 2 hours.

Make a creamy sauce as follows: Melt margarine in saucepan, add flour gradually, stirring all the time. Stir in about ½ pint of milk and liquid in which tripe was cooked. Cook a few minutes, then pour over tripe and onions.

This dish can be varied by omitting onions, and adding a few drops of tarragon vinegar to the sauce or 1 tablespoonful raw grated carrot.

THE REAL IRISH STEW

1 lb. middle or scrag end neck of mutton.	Equal quantities potatoes and onions.
1 teacupful water.	

Cut meat into neat chops, slice onions very thinly and cut potatoes in thick slices. Season well. Arrange in layers in saucepan, pour in water to cover and cook slowly 2½–3 hours. When ready, potatoes and onions should be a thick puree, with no liquid gravy.

TOAD-IN-THE-HOLE

½ lb. sausages.	1 egg or equivalent in egg
4 ozs. flour.	substitute.
Pinch salt.	½ pint milk.

Put flour and salt into a basin, make a well in centre. Break egg into it, stir in flour gradually, adding half the milk and beating well. (If substitute is used, mix with flour and salt before adding milk.) Add rest of milk. Let batter stand at least 1 hour before using. Scald sausages, remove skins and cut in halves. Grease a tin or pie dish, place sausages in it, season with pepper and salt, pour the batter over, and bake in a good oven till nicely browned and well risen, about 25–30 minutes.

Butcher's "Sundries"

BRAISED SWEETBREADS

Sweetbreads.	Thyme, parsley, salt, pepper.
Carrots, onions, bacon rind.	per.
1½ oz. flour or cornflour.	Stock or water.

First blanch sweetbreads as follows: Soak at least 1 hour in cold water, changing water from time to time. Then place in a stewpan, cover with cold water and bring slowly to boil. Cook gently 2 or 3 minutes. Remove them to a basin of cold water and wash well.

To braise, cover bottom of casserole with pieces of bacon rind, sliced onions and carrots, seasoning of pepper and salt, flavouring of thyme and parsley, and lastly the sweetbreads. Place lid on casserole and cook for a few minutes before adding sufficient stock or water to cover. Cook for about $\frac{3}{4}$–1 hour in fairly hot oven. Remove bacon rind before serving. A rasher of fat bacon cut in strips may be used instead of rind.

Mix flour or cornflour smoothly with a little cold milk or water, then add to liquid, which must be boiling. Simmer for not less than 3 minutes.

CALF'S LIVER BRAISED

1 lb. calf's liver.	1 oz. dripping or margarine.
2 rashers fat bacon	
2 carrots.	$\frac{1}{2}$ teaspoonful mixed herbs
1 turnip.	Pepper and salt to taste.
1 onion.	1 tumblerful water or stock
2 tomatoes or 2 tablespoonfuls tomato pulp.	

Fry all vegetables except tomatoes in dripping or margarine till a light golden brown. Add herbs and tomatoes. Place vegetables in casserole. Put in liver (in piece, not sliced) on top, add seasoning, and pour over water or stock. Allow 1 hour for slow stewing. A dash of sharp sauce of the Worcester or Yorkshire relish type added before serving gives piquancy. Serve mashed potatoes with this dish.

HARICOT OF OXTAIL

1 oxtail.	A stick or two of celery.
1 oz. flour.	Bouquet garni.
1 oz. dripping.	A little ground mace
2 onions (1 stuck with 2 cloves).	A few peppercorns
	Salt.
2 small turnips.	1 quart of water
2 medium-sized carrots	

Cut oxtail in sections. Melt dripping in stewpan, fry

oxtail and one onion sliced, till browned. Add flour and let it brown. Add water, stirring till well mixed and smooth, then vegetables cut up, onion stuck with cloves, herbs, spices and seasonings. Cook gently 3 to 4 hours.

Small haricot beans, soaked overnight in the usual way and cooked separately, are served with the haricot.

KIDNEY CASSEROLE

¾ lb. ox kidney.	Pepper, salt.
2 onions.	Flour.
2 lbs. potatoes.	Stock or water.
1 oz. cooking fat.	

Wash and dry kidney, cut in small pieces, dredge with flour, pepper, salt. Slice vegetables, brown them in fat in pan, then do same with kidney. Place alternate layers of kidney, onion and potatoes in casserole. Flavour well with pepper, salt and, if liked, a sprinkling of powdered sage. Add a little flour to fat in pan, also stock or water. Bring to boil and pour over contents of casserole. Put on lid. Cook in moderate oven 2 hours.

TONGUE MOULD TO SERVE COLD

3 sheep's tongues	1 bayleaf, pepper and salt
½ oz. gelatine.	to taste.
	Stock (about 1 pint).

Let tongues cook in salted water with bayleaf till tender, and then remove bones, skin and fat. Cut into thin slices. Dissolve gelatine in stock which has been seasoned to taste. Arrange slices of tongue in wetted mould or basin, and pour stock over them. Liquid

should be sufficient to cover slices. Turn out when set.
Garnish with sprigs of parsley, sliced tomatoes and beetroot.

This makes a nice cold supper or breakfast dish.

OX HEART, FORCEMEAT AND APPLE SAUCE

Enough ox heart sliced for 4 persons

For Forcemeat

2 rashers fat bacon.	1 tablespoonful parsley.
4 ozs. breadcrumbs.	½ teaspoonful mixed herbs
2 tablespoonfuls chopped suet or melted margarine.	Pinch of mace.
1 small onion.	Salt and pepper.
	Milk to bind.

To make forcemeat balls: Chop bacon and onion, add
other ingredients and mix with milk. Place ox heart and
balls in baking tin with 3 or 4 tablespoonfuls dripping.
Baste well. Bake in moderate oven 1½ hours.

Make apple sauce, serve gravy and sauce with dish.

SPICED COWHEEL AND BEEF MOULD

This cheap and nourishing dish is served cold with
salad.

½ cowheel.	Salt, pepper.
½ lb. leg of beef.	Parsley or watercress
Grated nutmeg or mace.	

Put beef and cowheel (ready dressed) into a saucepan
with cold water to cover. Add grated nutmeg or mace,
pepper and salt. Bring to boil, simmer slowly till
tender, about 3 hours. Remove beef and cowheel, chop
the whole not too finely ; put into basins or moulds
which have been rinsed in cold water. When quite set
turn out, garnish with parsley or watercress, and serve
with salad. Cut in fair-sized slices or wedges when
serving.

Every Housewife should know–

this Important Wartime Food Economy

EVERY housewife today recognizes the vital necessity for food economy. At the same time, it is of paramount importance to ensure that the family dietary is completely nourishing and health-giving.

Care must be taken to see that your meals provide all the food elements required to make good the present-day demands on body, brain and nerves. You will be greatly assisted in achieving this purpose if you make delicious "Ovaltine" the regular daily beverage for every member of the family.

"Ovaltine" is, in itself, a complete and perfect form of health-giving nourishment. It provides, in a concentrated and correctly balanced form, the nutritive elements necessary for good health and vitality. Moreover, "Ovaltine" possesses exceptional nerve-restoring properties which are due to the nature and high quality of its constituents and the exclusive scientific methods of manufacture. Obviously no food beverage can be fully restoring unless this property is derived from its ingredients.

"Ovaltine" is exceptionally economical in use and very easy to prepare. If milk is not available water can be used as "Ovaltine" itself contains milk. Moreover, as "Ovaltine" is naturally sweet there is no need to add sugar. "Ovaltine" can also be eaten dry if desired.

Spend wisely–
drink
Ovaltine
for Health

B

Meat Pie Making

COUNTRY HOUSE PIE

An old bird (grouse, partridge or other game).	2 ozs. chopped mushrooms
½ lb. steak.	1 rasher fat bacon.
1 chopped onion	½ pint stock, seasoning.
	Rough puff pastry.

Cut steak into small slices and place in bottom of a pie dish, seasoning well. Joint bird neatly; in the case of grouse remove lower portion of the back, as this gives a bitter flavour. Lay portions of bird on steak in pie dish, sprinkle on chopped bacon, onion and mushrooms. Fill up with stock made from trimmings and bones to about three-quarters of the depth of pie dish. Put lid on, simmer ½ hour.

Take dish out of oven, remove lid, allow to cool. Cover pie with pastry and return to hot oven, afterwards reduce heat a little.

INDIVIDUAL MUTTON PIES

¾ lb. lean mutton.	½ lb. flour.
1 onion.	2 ozs. margarine.
Parsley, seasoning, pinch nutmeg.	2 ozs. lard.
	Water.

To make pastry put flour and a pinch of salt into basin, rub in margarine and lard till mixture is like breadcrumbs. Make hollow in centre of flour, add enough water to form stiff paste. Turn on floured board and knead till free from cracks.

Cut mutton in small pieces, season with pepper, salt, nutmeg, add onion chopped small, and chopped parsley, mix with a little water to moisten.

Line patty tins with paste, fill with prepared meat, moisten with water or gravy. If shallow tins are used, the pastry lids should be a little larger than the linings. Make small hole in top of each pie and brush over with milk. Bake in moderate oven about 30 minutes.

RAISED SAUSAGE AND BACON PIE

½ lb. sausages.
2 ozs. fat bacon.
¼ teaspoonful mixed herbs
Salt and pepper

2 tablespoonfuls water or gravy.
½ gill water and 1 tablespoonful gelatine.

For Crust

6 ozs. flour.
1½ ozs. lard, pinch of salt.

¼ gill milk and water mixed.

Add salt to flour. Put lard with milk and water into a saucepan and bring to boil, stirring from time to time. Pour liquid into hollow in centre of flour, and work in flour with wooden spoon. Bind to stiff dough, kneading when cooled a little. Take ⅔rds of the crust, knead till free of cracks, then roll out and line bottom and sides of small pie tin with straight sides (cake tin will do).

Remove sausage skins and flake meat into dish. Fill up pie with layers of sausage meat and chopped bacon, adding seasoning, 2 tablespoonfuls water or gravy, and a few mixed herbs. Roll out remaining pastry for lid, and cover pie. Make an opening in centre. Cook in hot oven 50 minutes, and serve.

If required cold, melt gelatine in water over heat, pour liquid into pie through funnel. Leave to set.

SEA PIE

Any uncooked meat may be used. Cut up meat, arrange in casserole with alternate layers of vegetables such as sliced onion, carrot, shredded celery. Add a little chopped parsley, mixed herbs, pepper, salt, also sufficient stock or water to cover. Place lid on casserole and when contents have reached boiling point, simmer gently ½ hour.

Remove lid and place on top of meat and vegetables a light suet crust, cut to exact size of dish so that it fits inside, using for a medium-sized dish 8 ozs. self-raising flour, 4 ozs. shredded suet, salt, and water to mix.

Replace lid of casserole and cook another 1½ hours. Before serving, cut paste into triangular pieces.

SQUAB PIE WITH NECK OF MUTTON

This kind of pie belongs to the same family as the better-known Cornish pasty and hails from the West Country.

1½ lbs. neck of mutton	Pastry to cover.
1½ lbs. of apples.	Pork may be used instead
½ lb. onions finely chopped.	of mutton, in which case
2 teaspoonfuls sugar.	add 1 teaspoonful sage
Pepper and salt to taste.	and omit sugar.

Fill up pie dish, beginning with mutton cut into neat short chops. Sprinkle with chopped onion and seasoning. Next put layer of sliced apple sprinkled with sugar and if liked a little allspice. Continue with layers. See that last layer is of apples. Pour on a little water to keep contents moist, cover with pastry. If apples are tart, quantity of sugar should be increased.

A suitable pastry for squab pie has as its ingredients 1 lb. flour, ¼ lb. lard, 1 teaspoonful baking powder, salt to taste.

VENISON PIE

1½ lbs. venison, neck, breast or shoulder.	A little flour.
	Pepper, salt.
2 or 3 rashers fat bacon.	½ pint stock or water.
1 finely chopped onion.	Forcemeat.
½ teaspoonful mixed spice.	Pastry.

For Forcemeat

4 ozs. breadcrumbs.	1 teaspoonful mixed herbs.
2 ozs. chopped suet or 2 tablespoonfuls melted margarine.	Pinch of nutmeg.
	A little milk to mix.
1 tablespoonful chopped parsley.	The addition of a little mushroom or liver minced is an improvement.
1 teaspoonful grated onion.	

Wipe venison well, cut into small pieces. Mix flour, spice and seasoning, dip meat into mixture. Fill pie dish with venison, forcemeat, onion and chopped bacon, having forcemeat on top. Pour on stock or water. Put on lid or greased paper and cook in moderate oven for $1\frac{1}{2}$ hours. Then remove pie, let it cool, add more stock or water if required. Cover, when cool, with pastry. Return to hot oven till pastry has risen, then lower temperature. Cook second time $1\frac{1}{2}$ hours.

CHAPTER IV

REGIONAL SAVOURY PUDDINGS
SAVE MEAT

REGIONAL savoury puddings make a noteworthy chapter in the story of British domestic cookery . They were essential to economical catering in the large-family days of the great Victorian era because they saved meat without underfeeding. Once again they attract the housewife because they make a little meat go a long way. The appeal of haggis, chieftain of the pudding race, is peculiar to Scotsmen, though many collateral members of the haggis clan in black and white puddings have local fame in English counties. There is a rich choice of simple savoury puddings associated, in the first instance, with individual counties, which have become recognised national fare.

The old recipes have been adapted to conform with present-day conditions when food is lighter, eggs used with more restraint and the time of the cook is saved by recourse to ingredients ready for use—self-raising flour, shredded suet and a variety of bottled flavourings.

Most popular of all puddings partnering meats is that of Yorkshire, and next comes the Norfolk dumpling.

NORFOLK DUMPLINGS

½ lb. flour.
2–3 ozs. chopped suet
Pinch of salt.

Water, sufficient to mix into stiff paste

The original Norfolk dumpling had dough as its basis, but the above recipe is suited to modern requirements and gives a light, satisfying dumpling with boiled beef and carrots or dropped into stew which has come to boiling point. Mix ingredients well together and form into round balls. Allow ¾ hour for cooking or rather less if dumplings are kept small.

Many changes may be rung on this plain suet pudding or dumpling formula. It may be flavoured with mixed herbs or chopped onion, part breadcrumbs used in place of all flour, steamed whole in greased basin, or the basin lined with paste and filled with chopped root vegetables and gravy. An onion pudding is very savoury. Season the chopped onion and flavour with a little powdered sage or a couple of small leaves of the fresh herb.

Some modern cooks have experimented with tomato juice or pulp as ingredient. This type of savoury pudding opens out an interesting field for research work in home kitchen.

NORTH COUNTRY HERB PUDDING

This savoury pudding is associated with Cumberland and is served at its best in the spring-time when the variety of green things cultivated and wild is greatest, but there is a sufficient choice of greens to make it a possible all-the-year-round pudding.

2 lbs. mixed greens.
1 cupful barley.
1 cupful oatmeal.

A little chopped onion.
1–2 ozs. margarine.
Seasoning to taste.

Chop greens (include some spinach if possible), mix with the barley and oatmeal, tie up in cloth and soak in cold water overnight. Next day add chopped onion, margarine and seasoning, mix all well together. Press into greased basin and cook for 1½–2 hours.

Addition of a beaten egg improves this pudding. If preferred, pudding may be baked in greased pie dish in oven.

PEASE PUDDING

1 pint dried peas.	1 oz. margarine
Pepper and salt to taste	

Some peas require to be soaked overnight, other kinds can be cooked without this preliminary. Inquire when buying or, if in packet form, read directions. Tie peas in pudding cloth or muslin, leaving room for expansion, and boil in same liquid as pork till soft. Strain through colander, beat well with margarine and seasoning. Serve hot. This is a quick method. A better method, however, is to cook further by turning well-beaten pudding into greased basin, tying down and steaming till pudding is set firmly.

One variation is to use ⅓rd mashed potatoes to ⅔rds peas. It is surprising that this cheap and good savoury pudding does not appear more frequently at the family table. Once it becomes known the cook wonders why it should be exclusive to boiled pork. It need not be ; try it with boiled beef, with sausages, rashers of fat bacon grilled or fried, liver fried or cooked with onions or tomatoes.

YORKSHIRE PUDDING

¼ lb. flour.	1 egg.
½ pint milk.	Pinch of salt.

These ingredients are given in the proportions found to give best results, but the milk can be diluted with water up to half and half and sour milk used. Sour milk makes a lighter pudding ; if possible the batter should be mixed some time before pudding is poured into hot fat in dripping tin. Yorkshire pudding requires a hot oven.

There are different ways of mixing, but this is the simplest. Salt the flour in basin, break 1 egg into a well in centre and beat until flour is absorbed, adding the milk gradually. Batter should be smooth and sufficiently liquid to pour into the tin.

Tradition lays down that this pudding should be cooked under the roast beef and so absorb the rich meat juice that comes from joint, but it is a good dish in itself served with well-seasoned brown gravy.

CHAPTER V

SNACK FOOD FOR ANY HOUR

EVERY housewife and cook should be able to produce something in the way of the snack food now often wanted at little or no notice. Making of piquant spreads has become an important phase of homecraft and many novel fillings for sandwiches and additions to plain biscuits or toasted bread can be provided at small cost. Often practically all the ingredients can be found among "left overs" from the larder and so save waste. Some of the spreads used as fillings in pastry cases reheated in oven solve the problem of an inexpensive light luncheon dish.

SNACKS

Kedgeree.—Mix thoroughly ½ lb. rice cooked as for curry, ½ cupful flaked cooked dried haddock and 2 ozs. margarine. Season well—a grate of nutmeg is sometimes liked—and stir in a beaten egg. Heat through and when kedgeree is hot, pile on a dish and serve with oatcakes.

Walnut Patties.—Fill small pastry cases with a mixture made from 2 pickled walnuts, 1 hard-boiled egg, a little margarine and seasoning. If wanted hot, reheat cases.

Sausage Rissoles.—Mix ½ lb. mashed potatoes with ½ lb. skinned sausages, 1 oz. oatmeal, 1 small onion chopped, ½ teaspoonful sage, pepper and salt, and enough hot milk to make a pliable mixture. Shape into rissoles, dust over with oatmeal and fry till crisp and brown.

Welsh Rarebit.—Grate or shred 3 ozs. cheese and put in saucepan containing small piece of margarine. Add a dash of pepper, ¼ teaspoonful made mustard and a pinch of salt (if cheese is salt, more may not be advisable). Mix with about ¾ tablespoonful milk. Let ingredients simmer, stirring until cheese is melted. Pour on toasted or crisply dried pieces of stale bread and put under grill to brown.

Fish Sausages.—Pound well together 1 cupful fish and 1 cupful breadcrumbs or mashed potato. Mix in ½ oz. melted margarine or dripping, a dash of anchovy sauce, and seasoning. Bind with an egg or milk. Shape mixture into sausages, flour and fry.

Savoury Pancake.—Stuff pancake with any savoury compound of left-overs seasoned, mixed with a little stock or milk, and warmed in saucepan. Fry pancake, turn and add mixture before folding.

Stuffed Celery.—Mix together 3 ozs. grated cheese, 1 tablespoonful wholemeal breadcrumbs, ½ teaspoonful made mustard, ½ oz. margarine, a few drops Worcester or tomato sauce or vinegar, seasoning to taste. Prepare short lengths of white celery and stuff them with the mixture. Garnish with a little of green leaf of celery.

TOMATO TARTLETS

4 ozs. flour.	Cold water.
2 ozs. margarine.	Salt and pepper.
2 ozs. grated cheese.	

For Filling

2 small tomatoes.	A little salad cream or
4 gherkins.	mayonnaise.

Make savoury pastry by cutting and rubbing margarine

into flour, adding seasoning and cheese. Mix to a stiff consistency with cold water. Roll out thinly and line small shallow tins with the mixture. Cut the scraps of pastry into strips, place a strip across each patty tin to divide case in half. Bake in a moderate oven till golden brown. Allow to cool.

Chop gherkins finely and fill one half of each pastry case. Cut tomatoes into small dice; mix with salad cream. Fill the rest of the cases with this mixture.

SKINLESS SAUSAGES

These make a substantial snack dish or may be served for breakfast or luncheon and are good hot or cold.

1 cupful chopped or minced meat, fat and lean.	Herbs and seasoning to taste.
1 cupful breadcrumbs, white or wholemeal.	1 yolk of egg beaten.

Mix all ingredients well together, using plenty of pepper, but going sparingly with salt, as the breadcrumbs are salted. Flavouring is a matter of taste and depends to some extent on the meat.

If pork is used, marjoram and sage with a little mace are recommended. Thyme goes well with other meats, or one of the home-made herb mixtures from the store-cupboard may be used. Shape into sausages, flour and fry in hot fat.

A mixture of this kind may be made into tiny sausages and served cold at a snack meal, or it is suitable for sausage roll filling.

Small sausage rolls that can be eaten as finger food are preferred.

NOW

a limited supply again of

MACONOCHIE'S

Vegetables

in gravy

✦

Most good shops have a stock
but housewives who know how rich
and nourishing a meal they make
won't leave them there for long!

Don't miss this chance!

MACONOCHIE : BROS : LIMITED   LONDON

OATMEAL AND MEAT MOULD

A useful dish for all times, breakfast, luncheon, high tea, supper or snack.

1 breakfastcupful chopped cold meat (fat and lean, removing skin and gristle).	⅓rd breakfastcupful oatmeal.
1 tablespoonful shredded suet if meat is very lean.	½ small teaspoonful each salt and pepper.
⅔rds breakfastcupful brown and white breadcrumbs.	½ teaspoonful thyme.
	1 teaspoonful parsley.
	1 egg, a little milk.
	1 or 2 rashers of bacon.

Mix all ingredients well together and blend with beaten egg, adding milk if necessary. Grease a plain mould, placing a thin rasher at the bottom, allowing the two ends to come up sides of basin. A second rasher may be halved and wrapped round sides. Fill basin with mixture, pressing it down but leaving space for oatmeal to swell, say ¾ of an inch from top. Tie down with greaseproof paper and steam for 1¼ hours.

Mould may be turned out at once if wanted as a hot dish. If to be eaten cold, place small plate inside basin and a weight on top.

SPREADS

Anchovy Spread.—Pound 6 anchovies, from which the bones have been removed, with 1½ ozs. margarine. Add pepper, but no salt.

Cheese Spread.—Blend together grated cheese with a little made mustard to taste. Moisten with vinegar or Worcester sauce. Addition of a nut of margarine is optional.

Curry Spread.—Slightly melt 3 ozs. margarine, work in 2 teaspoonfuls curry powder. A sprinkling of mustard and cress with this spread is recommended.

Fish Paste.—Beat up mashed potato and sardines (in proportion of 1 dessertspoonful potato to 1 sardine), season well and moisten with vinegar.

Horseradish Spread.—Mix 1 tablespoonful finely grated horseradish with 2 ozs. margarine and a few drops of vinegar.

Liver and Bacon Paste.—Bring ½ lb. liver to boil with ½ teaspoonful allspice and 1 small onion chopped finely. Simmer 5 minutes. Put liver, and ¼ lb. fat from American bacon through mincer several times till mixture is smooth.

Meat Paste.—When braising steak for casserole or preparing it for pudding or pie, cut off 1½–2 ozs., cook gently, and pound with half its weight in margarine, pepper, salt and a grate or two of nutmeg or a pinch of mace.

Salmon Spread.—Beat into a smooth paste ¼ lb. tinned salmon, a sprinkling of breadcrumbs, pepper, salt, 1 teaspoonful grated nutmeg and 1 oz. margarine. Put into small jars. Will keep for a week.

HOT TOASTS

Kipper Toast.—Grill kipper, free from bone and skin, pound with 1 oz. margarine, dessertspoonful of breadcrumbs and pepper to season. Serve on hot toast.

Potato Cheese.—Cook together 1 tablespoonful finely grated horseradish, 1½ tablespoonfuls grated cheese, 1 tablespoonful milk, ½ teaspoonful pepper and salt mixed. Thicken with 1 tablespoonful mashed potato. Serve hot on rounds of fried bread or on oatcakes made hot.

Fried Bread Savouries.—Cut fried bread, crisp and piping hot, into slices, rounds, triangles or fingers. Pile on some savoury mixture—remainders of fish mixed with a little plain white sauce and lightly browned under the grill, pounded soft roes, a few sardines made hot, a little chopped American ham seasoned with made mustard, or cooked smoked haddock mixed with a little grated cheese and seasoned with cayenne pepper, are suggestions

CHAPTER VI

COOKING FROM THE
GARDEN

ONE of the happiest alliances in catering is that between
the cook and the kitchen gardener working in the interests
of good fare, the former delighting in making the best
use of fresh vegetables and fruits, and the gardener growing not so much for the exhibition stand as for the
requirements of the cook.

In these days many home cooks combine the two roles,
cultivating their own vegetables, salads and herbs.   This
seems an ideal plan, for the cook-gardener will know the
exact time when a vegetable has arrived at the best
moment for cooking or storing.   All green vegetables
depend for perfection on their freshness.

Seven Phases of Carrot

More ways of serving root vegetables are being worked
out in the kitchen.   Carrots have come to occupy a new
place in cookery—grated raw, steamed, boiled, stewed,
whole, in the form of puree, or cut into rounds or elegant
tapering points.   They go into sweet puddings, tarts and
preserves, give both substance and colour to soups and
sauces, and are even a decoration for the table ; small
dishes of grated or shredded carrot bring a glow of rich
colour, and if any should be left over it can go into soup
or stew.

Turnip—Root and Tops

Turnips and young swedes demand little in the way of
treatment beyond cooking till tender and the addition of a

piece of margarine, pepper and salt. A pretty dish can be produced by the cook who serves turnip tops chopped and seasoned with the white roots thickly sliced, dressing with a white sauce or seasoned melted margarine.

Swede Cakes

A good dish is made by mixing well together 1 cupful of well-drained mashed swedes with 1 cupful of mashed potatoes, 2 teaspoonfuls of melted margarine or dripping and seasoning to taste. Form into flat cakes, flour and fry golden brown. Serve alone or with a sausage or a rasher of bacon to each cake.

Sausages and Parsnips

Parsnips, steamed, boiled, baked, mashed and made into savoury cakes for frying or baking, or as fritters, go well with most meats or may be served alone. Try these also with sausages as an economical main dish, or with liver and bacon.

Artichokes and Salsify

Good soups and a selection of inexpensive dishes of the au gratin or scalloped class are possible when Jerusalem artichokes are available. A few drops of vinegar should be added to the water in which artichokes and salsify are boiled. This keeps them white.

All-In Celery

Celery when it comes into the kitchen is one of the most hard-working of vegetables—root, stalk and branch. Raw, it contributes to a variety of mixed salads, or is curled with the cheese ; it flavours soups, goes into casserole and stew, or with a white sauce flavoured to taste is a dish in itself.

ARTICHOKE SAVOURY

2 lbs. Jerusalem artichokes   3 or 4 tablespoonfuls gra-
1½ ozs. margarine.   ted cheese.
1 oz. flour.   ½ pint milk.
    Seasoning, browned breadcrumbs, cayenne, vinegar.

Wash and peel artichokes. To preserve colour, put
them when peeled into cold water to which a little
vinegar has been added. Cook for about 30 minutes in
boiling water to which vinegar is also added. Drain,
grease a pie dish or casserole, put in the artichokes cut in
thick slices, and cover with cheese sauce. Sprinkle with
a few browned breadcrumbs and a little cayenne, and put
on top a few pats of margarine.

To make cheese sauce : Melt 1 oz. margarine in
saucepan, add flour, cook a minute or two without
browning. Add milk gradually, stirring well. Cook
2 minutes, add cheese, stir till cheese is melted.

BACON AND SPROUTS

1 lb. Brussels sprouts.   ½ gill stock (can be made
2 or 3 rashers chopped fat   from meat extract).
    bacon.   Flour, parsley, salt, pepper,
½ oz. margarine.   pinch of nutmeg.
1 chopped onion.

Cook sprouts in boiling salted water 15 to 30 minutes,
according to size. Drain, sprinkle with flour. Melt
margarine in pan, put in bacon, fry a few minutes, add
onion and cook till lightly brown. Stir in seasoning,
nutmeg and stock. Add sprouts, stir till they have
absorbed gravy. Serve garnished with chopped parsley.

BAKED PARSNIPS

1 lb. parsnips.   Seasoning.
1 oz. dripping or margarine.   Parsley.

Scrape parsnips and parboil whole in salted water.

Drain, cut into quarters or 2-inch rounds, put into dish with joint about 30 minutes before meat is cooked. Alternatively put in baking tin in which a little fat has been melted. Sprinkle with pepper, finish cooking and brown in oven. Garnish with chopped parsley. Serve very hot with meat, roast or grilled, fried bacon or sausages.

CAULIFLOWER FRITTERS

Cauliflower.	Parsley.
Plain seasoned batter (may be made with egg substitute).	Cayenne pepper.

Prepare the cauliflower, and half cook in salt and water. Break off the flowerets and dip into batter, fry them golden brown. Garnish with sprigs of fresh green parsley and dust over with cayenne pepper.

The remainder of the cauliflower can be used in making cauliflower cream soup.

GREEN PEAS AND CARROTS

1 lb. shelled green peas.	1 tablespoonful flour.
1 lb. small young carrots	Seasoning.
1 oz. margarine.	

Scrape carrots, cut in halves, put into saucepan with a little water. Cook 10–15 minutes, then add peas and cook another 15 minutes or till peas are tender. If vegetables become too dry add a little more water, which must be boiling, but it is better for them to cook in steam and their own juice. When cooked, put in margarine, dredge flour over them to thicken, season, and add gradually boiling water to make sauce.

MIXED VEGETABLE STEW—WHITE OR BROWN

White

Small onions, celery, cauliflower cut in sprigs, young carrots, marrow, young turnips, potatoes.	Thyme, parsley, marjoram. Salt, pepper. Margarine. Left-overs of meat.

Arrange prepared vegetables in layers in greased casserole, sprinkle with herbs, season. Any left-overs of veal, lamb or poultry can be used for one of the layers. Add enough water to prevent burning. Dot with margarine. Simmer in closely covered casserole till cooked. Serve with white sauce poured over, using vegetable liquid to make sauce.

Brown

Vegetables as above Tomatoes. Beef or game left-overs 1 tablespoonful flour.	Margarine. Pickled walnuts, sage mushroom ketchup. Seasoning.

Fry onions first. Then other vegetables, and place in casserole with "left-overs". Season between layers and sprinkle over layers sage and mushroom ketchup. Add flour to fat in pan, cook till brown, add a little water, cook a few minutes till gravy thickens slightly. Add to vegetables in casserole. Cook till tender. Serve with pickled walnuts.

MOCK GOOSE

1 medium-sized vegetable marrow. 2 ozs. sausage meat. 2 ozs. breadcrumbs. 2 ozs. chopped onion.	½ teaspoonful powdered or chopped sage. Pepper, salt. Milk or egg.

Cut marrow into two, lengthwise. Remove seeds. Make stuffing by mixing well in basin sausage meat.

breadcrumbs, onion, sage and seasoning. Bind with a little milk or beaten egg. Press stuffing well into cavities, bring two parts of marrow together, tie with string. Place marrow in greased baking tin, bake till tender, $\frac{1}{2}$ to $\frac{3}{4}$ hour. Remove string. Serve with brown gravy and potatoes.

SPINACH SHAPE

Spinach.	1 egg.
Breadcrumbs.	Seasoning.

Prepare the spinach and cook till tender. Drain and extract all the water, and pass through a wire sieve. Take equal quantities of this puree and breadcrumbs and mix well together, adding seasoning. Bind with a beaten egg. Fill a greased mould with the mixture, steam 1 hour.

Serve with a simple sauce or a dish of gravy. This provides either a complete course or an accompaniment with grilled cutlet, sausages, sauted kidneys, etc.

STUFFED CABBAGE

1 cabbage, 1 onion, 1 carrot sliced.	$\frac{3}{4}$ pint stock or water.
1 oz. margarine.	2 tablespoonfuls tomato juice.
1 oz. flour.	Pepper, salt.

For Stuffing

$\frac{1}{2}$ lb. sausage meat or any left-over cold meat, minced.	Chopped onion. Pinch of spice. Salt, pepper.
3 tablespoonfuls breadcrumbs.	Milk to bind.

Wash and remove outside leaves from cabbage. Blanch it by pouring boiling water over. Drain off all water. Cut out stalk end, making a hollow shell. Put into basin the sausage meat, breadcrumbs, chopped onion, spice and seasoning, and bind with a little milk. Pack into cabbage.

Melt margarine in saucepan, add flour and seasoning, stir in stock or water and tomato flavouring and make a smooth liquid sauce. Place cabbage in this, together with a sliced onion and carrot. Cover pan and simmer $1\frac{1}{2}$ hours.

TOMATO PIE

$\frac{1}{4}$ lb. rice.
1 lb. tomatoes.
2 onions.
Dripping, margarine.
Parsley.

Seasoning.
Cheese sauce (*see* "Arti-
choke Savoury").
Grated cheese.

Boil rice, strain and dry. Fry sliced onions and tomatoes in a little dripping. Mix in pie dish with rice, chopped parsley, seasoning and cheese sauce. Sprinkle with grated cheese. Put in quick oven to brown.

VEGETABLE CURRY

Any cooked vegetables—carrots, turnips, peas, beans, potatoes, cauliflower.

For Curry Sauce

1 onion.
$1\frac{1}{2}$ ozs. dripping.
2 ozs. flour.
1 tablespoonful curry pow-
der.

2 teaspoonfuls curry paste.
2 chopped chillies.
1 pint water.
Salt.

Melt dripping in a saucepan, fry finely sliced onion, chillies, curry powder, flour and curry paste. Cook a few minutes, add water and salt. Simmer gently 30 minutes. Add the vegetables, well cooked but not too soft, and cut into small pieces. Stir till hot through. Serve with boiled rice.

Vita-Weat REGD

SPRINGS FROM BRITISH SOIL
—AND BUILDS UP BRITISH NERVE

From the golden wheatfields of Britain comes Vita-Weat, Peek Frean's famous crispbread. No ships are needed, no sailors' lives risked, to bring Vita-Weat to our shores. It contains the *whole* wheat germ, with its valuable Vitamin B1 content. Busy men and women are finding that Vita-Weat—so crisp, light and starch-free—is easy on the digestion, leaves the mind alert and clear, and helps the system to function regularly.

Vita-Weat
FEEK FREAN'S CRISPBREAD
Cartons 1/6 and 10d.
Packets 6d. and 2d.

Made by Peek Frean & Co. Ltd. Makers of Famous Biscuits

The Conquering Carrot

BAKED IN DRIPPING

Carrots.   Flour.
Dripping.

Boil the required number of carrots till tender, but
not too soft. Cut in slices or quarters lengthwise.
Remove from the water, drain and leave a minute or two
to dry. Sprinkle with flour. Meanwhile melt dripping
in a meat tin. When boiling hot throw in the carrots.
Cook in hot oven till brown and crisp, basting occasionally.

CREAMED CARROTS

1½ lbs. carrots.   ¼ pint milk and ¼ pint
1 oz. flour.   vegetable water (or ½ pint
1 oz. margarine.   vegetable water).
Pepper and salt.   Chopped parsley.

Wash and scrape carrots, cook in boiling salted water
20 minutes. Prepare white sauce by melting fat in
saucepan, stirring in flour smoothly, and adding liquid,
little by little. Stir till mixture is boiling, then simmer
2 or 3 minutes. Season with pepper and salt.

Stir white sauce into carrots, or pour over carrots on a
hot dish. Scatter over chopped parsley.

CURRIED CARROTS

Carrots.   1 oz. margarine or drip-
1½ teaspoonfuls curry pow-   ping.
  der.   1 onion.
3 teaspoonfuls flour.   ½ pint stock or water.
                                 Pepper and salt.

Trim carrots and boil in the usual way. Prepare
curry sauce as follows. Melt fat in saucepan, add onion
chopped, and fry a few minutes. Add curry powder

and flour and fry, stirring from time to time, for a few minutes longer. Stir in stock or water, and when boiling, season to taste. Simmer gently about 30 minutes.

Add cooked carrots to curry sauce in saucepan and cook 20–30 minutes. Serve with a garnish of cooked rice.

GOLDEN GLAZE

1 lb. carrots.	1 pint stock or water.
1 finely chopped onion.	A little meat extract.
2 ozs. margarine or dripping.	Mace or nutmeg.
	Pepper, salt
1 dessertspoonful chopped parsley.	1 oz. flour.

Melt 1 oz. margarine in saucepan. Put into it onion, carrots, pinch of nutmeg or mace, cook a few minutes to brown onion lightly. Add stock, parsley and seasoning. Simmer gently 35 minutes.

Meanwhile melt the remaining margarine in small pan, add flour. Stir till golden brown. When carrots are cooked, strain the liquid in which they have cooked into margarine and flour and stir till it boils. Pour over carrots, cook 5 or 6 minutes.

HOT RUSSIAN SALAD

12 small carrots.	1 teaspoonful castor sugar
1 pint green peas.	1 teaspoonful finely chopped mint.
¼ lb. bacon.	

Prepare peas and carrots, boil separately in slightly salted water, strain till dry. Cut bacon in cubes and fry in own fat, a golden brown.

Lightly mix bacon, peas and carrots which have been cut in half in lengths after cooking, with sugar and mint. Pour bacon fat over all. Serve very hot.

TWO-COLOUR SALAD

Cooked carrots.   Mayonnaise.
Watercress, parsley.   Seasoning.
Grated cheese.

Cut carrots in slices or dice, put into a salad bowl,
season with pepper and salt. Pour over a little mayonnaise, sprinkle with finely grated cheese and parsley,
garnish with the watercress washed and dried. This
salad looks most attractive—green and gold.

WHEN CARROTS ARE YOUNG

Young carrots.   Water.
Nut of margarine.   Salt.
1 teaspoonful sugar.   Chopped parsley.

Trim carrots and cook whole with just enough water
to cover, adding a pinch of salt, the fat and sugar ; do
not cover saucepan. By the time cooking is finished,
water will have boiled away. Serve carrots very hot,
sprinked with chopped parsley.

CHAPTER VII

POTATOES SOLVE MANY
PROBLEMS

FROM time to time we are assured on the word of
eminent chefs that there are one, two and even three
hundred ways of cooking the potato, and the British
housewife has been criticised for her conservatism in the
small number of methods in regular use in the home.
What is more to the point, our cooks have been taken to

task for their inability to cook potatoes satisfactorily even within the narrow limits of the methods they have chosen.

Some of this criticism is unfair. Potatoes boiled, steamed or baked in their jackets, roasted with the joint, fried to a pale golden brown crispness, or cold potatoes sauted represent the modest but excellent selection used in the ordinary home. Each one can present perfection in potato cookery.

To be eaten at its best, full of flavour and floury, the potato should not be allowed to go through its fiery ordeal, whether boiled, steamed or baked, in a state of nudity. Properly clothed in its own well-scrubbed jacket with just a narrow ribbon of the skin removed, it emerges perfect without waste in preparation. This is the way the plain baked potato appears at City livery luncheons.

Even when the potato is to be served mashed, this is a practical manner of cooking, for the skin may be peeled quickly and effectively before mashing.

There are more ways than one of mashing, and choice is governed largely by what the family prefers. There is the rather moist creamy mash produced by application with a wooden potato masher or the back of a wooden spoon, a little salt, melted margarine, or, if preferred, hot milk being worked in.

Many people like a lighter form of mashed potato when the vegetable is whisked into a state of fluffiness with the aid of a fork or forks, or, better still, passed through a wire sieve. A little salt is then the only addition.

The roasted or browned potato all sizzling and hot from its sojourn in the dripping-pan with the roast, the chipped potato, succulent within but crisp and richly brown outside, and the delicately sauted potato which makes a modern appeal, can each in turn represent the fine art of potato cookery. But potatoes require to be served at once ; if allowed to stand they become sad, and of bad colour.

BAKED STUFFED POTATOES

4 large potatoes.
1 medium-sized onion.
1½ tablespoonfuls gravy

Salt and pepper.
A few drops of mushroom
or tomato ketchup.

Peel potatoes evenly, cut off tops, about ¾ inch thick, hollow out centres. Parboil and chop onion, mix with scooped-out potato, season well, and moisten with gravy, adding ketchup to flavour. Fill potatoes with this mixture, replace tops, and bake for about 1 hour.

White sauce may be substituted for the gravy. Other variations include addition of tomato pulp, finely chopped left-overs of meat or poultry or sausage meat flavoured with herbs.

JULIENNE PIE

1 lb. cooked potatoes.
Warm milk or a little mar-
garine.
Pepper, salt.
Tomato sauce or gravy.

Vegetables in season—
carrots, celery, cabbage,
onions, French or run-
ner beans.

Sieve potatoes, season and mix to a cream with warm milk or margarine. Grease pie dish and use half of potato mixture to line it. Fill up dish with diced vegetables, pour over a little tomato sauce or gravy, season well. Cover with remaining potato, brush over top with milk, and bake in moderate oven till browned, about ¾–1 hour.

LYONNAISE

1¼ lb. cooked potatoes
¼ lb. onions
Dripping.

Pepper, salt.
Parsley.

Slice onions crosswise, and fry in fat till lightly browned. Slice potatoes, keeping slices whole, lightly saute in dripping. Serve potatoes, well seasoned with pepper and salt, on hot dish ; garnish with onion, and sprinkle chopped parsley over.

PATTIES WITH MEAT FILLING

1 lb. potatoes.	Hot milk.
2 tablespoonfuls medium oatmeal.	Finely chopped cold meat.
	Pepper and salt.

Mash potatoes with milk, whisking until very light and fluffy and working in gradually the oatmeal. Shape paste into thick rounds, scoop out a little from the centres, leaving a firm basis. Well season meat and fill into cavity, cover with scooped-out mixture, and fry till golden brown.

POTATO SPLITS

1 lb. mashed potatoes kept dry and fluffy.	Flour as required.
1½ ozs. margarine.	Pinch of salt.

Work margarine, salt and enough flour into potatoes to make a dough that can be rolled out on well-floured board. Flour rolling pin, roll out dough not more than $\frac{1}{3}$ an inch thick, and cut into fair-sized rounds. Bake quickly on floured oven sheet, turning cakes when browned on one side.

If there is mashed potato to be used up, these cakes are made in a few minutes. They can be split and eaten hot, or make a breakfast or supper dish with some simple savoury filling. Or they are good as a basis for serving baked beans and tomato, a grilled sausage, sardines made hot and seasoned with pepper and a few drops of vinegar. Toasted cheese, fried mushrooms or fried tomatoes are other ideas.

SAVOURY APPLE HOT-POT

6 apples.
6 potatoes.
2 onions.
½ lb. cooked meat.
Mixed herbs.

1 teaspoonful chopped parsley.
¼ pint stock or water
½ oz. margarine.

Cut apples and onions in small pieces, slice the potatoes. Put into greased casserole, alternate layers of potato, onion and apple, sprinkling layers with herbs and seasoning. Add stock or water, finish with a layer of potatoes. Put pats of margarine on top, bake in moderate oven till potatoes are well-browned—about ¾–1 hour.

SCALLOPED POTATOES

1 lb. potatoes, peeled.
1½ tablespoonfuls bread-crumbs.
1 tablespoonful chopped onion.

1 oz. margarine.
½ pint milk.
A little dripping.
Pepper and salt to taste.
Chopped parsley.

Grease fireproof glass or earthenware dish. Place layers of thinly sliced potatoes and of the onion, which is first lightly fried in dripping, in the dish, adding breadcrumbs and seasoning. Finish with layer of potatoes sprinkled with a few breadcrumbs which have been kept back. Put small dabs of margarine on top, pour milk over, and bake in moderate oven for ¾ hour or until potatoes are cooked. Garnish with chopped parsley.

For the Sweet Course

BAKED POTATO PUDDING

½ lb. smoothly mashed potato.
1½ ozs. castor sugar.
2 ozs. currants.
2 ozs. margarine.

Lemon substitute equivalent to 1 lemon.
1 egg.
Milk.

Cream fat and sugar, mix in mashed potato with well-beaten egg and sufficient milk to make a soft mixture. Add lemon substitute and currants, mix thoroughly, bake in greased pie dish in moderate oven $\frac{3}{4}$ hour.

CHEESE CAKES

3 heaped tablespoonfuls floury mashed potato.
1 tablespoonful currants.
1 tablespoonful castor sugar.
$\frac{1}{2}$ tablespoonful shredded candied peel.
1 oz. margarine.

1 egg well beaten.
A few drops of ratafia or almond flavouring or $\frac{1}{2}$ small teaspoonful grated nutmeg.
Little milk to mix.
Short pastry.

Mix dry ingredients, melt and add margarine and flavouring, beat all well together with egg and milk, as required. Half fill pastry-lined patty tins with mixture, which tends to rise in cooking, bake in quick oven about 15–20 minutes.

CHAPTER VIII

SALADS FOR ALL SEASONS

CHEESE SALAD

Cold boiled potatoes.
Grated cheese.
Salad cream.

1 small onion.
Beetroot, parsley.

Boil the potatoes in their skins, peel and slice them while hot. When cold mix with the finely chopped onion. Arrange in a salad bowl with layers of grated cheese. Add salad cream. Garnish with slices of beetroot and chopped parsley.

CUCUMBER SALAD

Peel cucumber and cut lengthwise or in slices. Soak in salted water ½ hour. Drain, dry and chop finely, then dress with seasoned oil and white vinegar, or a little vinegar from pickled onion jar. Sprinkle with chopped chervil or parsley.

HARICOT AND BACON SALAD

Haricot beans, cooked.	Chopped parsley
Cold fat bacon.	French dressing
Onion, tomato.	Pepper, salt

Rub salad bowl with clove of garlic. Then put in haricot beans, finely shredded onion, cold bacon cut in strips or diced, sliced tomatoes, add parsley and seasoning. Pour over a little French dressing—1 table-spoonful salad oil and 1 dessertspoonful white vinegar.

INDIAN SALAD

1 tin salmon, prawns, tunny fish or crayfish	1 dessertspoonful curry paste.
Lettuce or endive.	3 tablespoonfuls salad oil.
1 onion, 1 tomato	1 teaspoonful mango or home-made chutney.
A few capers.	A few drops vinegar
Cucumber.	

Chop onion, tomato and capers, put into a basin with chutney and mix thoroughly with curry paste, salad oil and vinegar. Add fish and mix. Serve on lettuce leaves in salad bowl, or on individual salad plates Garnish with sliced cucumber.

LENTIL SALAD

1 pint cooked lentils.	Small lettuce.
1 head celery, shredded.	Parsley.
1 tablespoonful finely chopped spring onion.	Dressing.

Mix lentils, celery and onion with salad dressing

BOVRIL
COOK'S TRUMP CARD

Good cooks have made good use of Bovril for over 50 years—
and today, when the health of the nation is so important, its
value in cooking is even greater than ever. Bovril not only
adds to enjoyment, but, by stimulating the powers of
assimilation, it enables you to get more benefit from other
food. For quality, there is nothing to equal it.

A little Bovril does wonders for the tastiness of any dish
—it brings out the flavour and gives an appetising goodness all
its own. Try it in stews and meat-pies—and don't forget
Bovril when making soups, sauce or gravy.

Always keep BOVRIL in the house

according to taste. Cover the salad bowl with lettuce leaves. Put the other ingredients on and sprinkle with finely chopped parsley.

SALAD LUNCHEON DISH

¼ lb. sliced luncheon sausage.
3 tablespoonfuls cold cooked diced potatoes.
2 tablespoonfuls cooked and sliced beetroot.
2 tablespoonfuls cooked carrots, diced.
Few slices finely shredded onion.
Garlic.
Lettuce dressing.

Rub the salad bowl with garlic, then put in all the salad ingredients and garnish with lettuce leaves. Moisten with French dressing.

MOCK WALDORF SALAD

1 cupful diced celery or grated celery root.
1 cupful diced apple.
½ cupful diced beetroot.
Parsley.
1 tablespoonful home-made salad cream.

Mix all well together, stir in salad cream, sprinkle with chopped parsley. If liked this salad may be served on lettuce or endive leaves.

SARDINE OR HERRING SALAD

Tin of sardines or tin of herrings.
1 tablespoonful capers.
1 lettuce.
3 or 4 cooked and sliced cold potatoes.
A few sprigs cooked cauliflower.
Beetroot, sliced.
Finely chopped parsley.

Remove skin and bones from sardines or herring, and divide into small pieces. Mix all ingredients in a salad bowl with dressing of oil and vinegar, sprinkle with chopped parsley.

SPRING GREEN SALAD

A tempting spring or summer accompaniment to cold mutton or lamb is a salad containing the familiar accompaniments of these meats—peas, new potatoes and mint.

Wash and shred young lettuce leaves lightly with fingers (do not cut), place in salad bowl. Dice some new potatoes, chop up 5 or 6 small spring onions, prepare 10 or 12 radishes, slice thinly a little cucumber if available. Add all to bowl with two tablespoonfuls cooked peas. Mix well with oil and vinegar dressing. Sprinkle with finely chopped mint.

If a salad accompaniment to cold beef is required, substitute sliced tomato for peas and garnish with finely grated horseradish in place of mint.

CHAPTER IX

HOT SAUCES

A GOOD BROWN SAUCE

½ pint gravy or water
1 onion.
A few small pieces carrot and turnip.
1 small tomato (optional)
Few sprigs parsley

Pinch of mixed herbs.
1 oz. dripping or margarine.
1 oz. flour.
Salt, pepper

Slice onion, carrot and turnip. Melt dripping in saucepan, brown onion, carrot and turnip in it, add flour and fry until brown. Add tomato sliced, parsley, herbs, seasoning, then stock gradually, stirring till sauce is smooth and creamy. Simmer gently 20 minutes. Strain.

This sauce will make a piquant accompaniment to pork, steak or cutlets by adding to ½ pint of it 1 dessertspoonful mushroom ketchup or 1 teaspoonful Worcester sauce, 1 small tablespoonful vinegar, simmer 20 minutes, then add 1 small teaspoonful made mustard.

MUSHROOM SAUCE TO GO WITH FISH

½ pint fish stock.
¼ pint milk.
4 chopped mushrooms or 1 dessertspoonful mushroom ketchup.
1 thinly sliced onion.

Bouquet garni or ½ teaspoonful mixed herbs.
1 oz. flour.
1 oz. margarine.
Salt, pepper, pinch nutmeg.

Make stock by putting fish bones and pieces into saucepan with a little over ½ pint water. Add chopped mushroom, sliced onion, herbs. Simmer 15–20 minutes.

In another saucepan melt margarine, add flour, mixing well, pour on milk gradually and cook a minute or two. Add the flavoured and strained fish stock, also the chopped mushrooms from stock, salt, pepper and pinch of nutmeg. Cook 2 or 3 minutes before serving.

ONION SAUCE

2 onions.
½ pint milk, or milk and water.
1 oz. flour.

1 oz. margarine.
Pepper, salt, pinch of nutmeg.

Boil onions till soft. Drain and chop. Melt margarine in saucepan, add flour, cook a little, but do not brown. Add milk gradually, stirring to make smooth. Cook till it boils, then stir in onions, salt, pepper and dash of nutmeg.

PARSLEY SAUCE.

1 oz. margarine.
1 oz. flour.
¾ pint milk or milk and water.

1 tablespoonful parsley. washed, dried and chopped.
Pepper, salt.

Melt margarine in pan, add flour, mix to a smooth paste. Cook a few minutes without browning. Add liquid very gradually, stirring, bring slowly to boiling point, simmer 2 or 3 minutes. Then season and lastly add chopped parsley, just before serving.

For caper sauce, substitute for parsley 1 tablespoonful chopped capers and a dash of vinegar. Add capers at the last minute, in the same way as parsley.

TIME-SAVING BREAD SAUCE

2 ozs. breadcrumbs.
½ pint milk.
1 small onion.

Pinch of pepper.
1 saltspoonful salt.
A dust of nutmeg

Simmer onion in milk for 15 minutes. Pour milk and onion over seasoned crumbs in basin. Cover with plate or lid and leave to keep hot on cooking stove till wanted. Just before serving, stir sauce lightly with fork. Serve with game, poultry, grilled cutlets, sausages or fried liver.

TOMATO AND CELERY SAUCE

5 tomatoes or 2 tablespoonfuls tomato pulp.
1 small onion.
Stick of celery.
½ teaspoonful castor sugar

Bouquet garni.
¾ oz. flour.
2 ozs. margarine.
½ pint stock or water.

Melt half the margarine in pan, put into it the sliced onion and celery cut in small pieces, fry a few minutes, then add sliced tomatoes, herbs, salt. Cover pan, cook 15 minutes over very gentle heat, stir in flour, add stock or water, mix thoroughly, boil together 15 minutes. Sieve, reheat and add rest of margarine, seasoning and sugar. Serve with fish or meat.

Sauce for the Sweet

CHOCOLATE SAUCE

3 teaspoonfuls chocolate or cocoa powder.	A little sugar.
2 teaspoonfuls cornflour.	½ pint milk.

Mix chocolate, sugar and cornflour with a little milk, cook 3 or 4 minutes, pour on rest of the milk and boil gently, stirring well.

ANOTHER METHOD :—

A simple chocolate sauce can be made with custard powder (vanilla flavour or unflavoured, in which case add a few drops vanilla essence), 2 ozs. grated chocolate and ½ pint milk, sugar to taste. Grate chocolate into small saucepan, add a little milk and cook a few minutes. Make custard in usual way, adding sugar if required, and pour on to melted chocolate, bring to boil.

SPICED SAUCE FOR CHRISTMAS PUDDING

This spiced sauce makes a good accompaniment to plum pudding.

½ oz. flour.	1 oz. sugar.
1 oz. margarine.	1 teaspoonful nutmeg or mixed spice.
½ pint milk, or milk and water.	

Melt margarine in saucepan, add flour, cook a few minutes. Add liquid by degrees, stirring all the time till mixture is smooth. Bring to boil, simmer a minute or two. Add nutmeg or spice and sugar. Stir well.

CHAPTER X

PUDDINGS AND SWEETS, HOT AND COLD

BAKED APPLES

Large cooking apples.   Margarine.
Sugar (brown preferably).

Wipe fruit carefully, remove small circle of peel from the top and core. Put a little sugar and a tiny piece of margarine into the cavity, stand apples in fireproof dish with small quantity of water, and bake in moderate oven till soft, about 1 hour.

Filling can be varied to taste. Other ideas are jam or mincemeat, or a few sultanas or raisins.

CHRISTMAS PUDDING WITHOUT EGGS

6 ozs. flour.
6 ozs. breadcrumbs.
1 lb. fruit (raisins, sultanas and currants mixed).
4 ozs. chopped or shredded suet.
4 ozs. sugar.
1 tablespoonful grated carrot.
½ teaspoonful baking powder.
½ teaspoonful ground ginger.
½ teaspoonful grated nutmeg.
Pinch of salt.
1 tablespoonful candied peel (optional).
Milk to mix.

Clean and pick over fruit, chop raisins. Mix ingredients well and leave to stand for 12 hours. Add a little milk to mix to stiff consistency, fill mixture into greased basin. Tie down with greased paper and floured pudding cloth. Steam for 6 hours.

As pudding is not made for long keeping this amount of cooking is sufficient, but another hour improves colour.

ANOTHER METHOD :—

6 ozs. flour.
6 ozs. breadcrumbs.
4 ozs. shredded suet.
1 lb. fruit (raisins, sultanas, currants).
3 ozs. sugar.
1 tablespoonful grated apple.

¾ teaspoonful baking powder.
½ nutmeg, grated.
½ teaspoonful mixed spice.
½ tumblerful stout.
Milk.

Prepare fruit, mix together dry ingredients. Moisten with the stout, adding milk as required. Mixture should be fairly stiff. Stir well, put into greased basin, tie down, leave for 12 hours, then steam for 7 hours.

FRUIT RICE

2 ozs. ground rice.
1 pint milk, or milk and water.
1 oz. sugar.

Pinch of salt.
Stewed or fresh fruit.

Bring milk to boil, sprinkle in ground rice and salt. Keep mixture well stirred, cooking till it is thick. Add sugar. Allow to cool till firm to the touch. Rinse shallow mould with water, line sides with rice mixture, bringing it right up to the top, and leaving a space in the centre. Fill up this space with fresh or stewed fruit. Chill mould, turn out just before required.

GOLDEN APPLE PUDDING

4 ozs. self-raising flour.
2 ozs. breadcrumbs.
3 ozs. margarine or suet.
2 tablespoonfuls golden syrup or honey.

2 apples.
1 egg.
A little milk.

Cut apples in dice and cook slightly in a little of the margarine. Put flour and breadcrumbs into basin, rub in rest of margarine or finely grated suet, add fried apple, syrup melted in warmed milk, then the egg well beaten. Mix thoroughly and put into greased basin. Steam 1½ hours.

MERINGUES

2 ozs. castor sugar.
1 egg white.
Vanilla or coffee essence

Custard filling. (*See* "War-time Eclairs.")

Beat egg white very stiff. Fold in sugar with a tablespoon and add flavouring to taste. Put preparation in forcing bag and press on to greased baking tin small oval portions, or take up a small dessertspoonful meringue mixture in a wet spoon and scoop it out with another spoon or palette knife. Dredge with a little castor sugar. Bake in very cool oven for 1½ hours till crisp. Turn them over and scoop out any portion that has not hardened and leave in warm place till dry. Spread the filling thickly on the cases, and place them together in pairs.

MIXED FRUIT ROLL

8 ozs. flour.
4 ozs. finely chopped suet.
¼ teaspoonful baking pow-
der.
Water

Mixed fruit.
Mixed spice.
1 tablespoonful golden syrup.
Pinch of salt.

Mix flour, salt, baking powder and suet with enough water to make a smooth soft dough, knead lightly with hands. Roll out into oblong shape about ¼ inch thick, spread with chopped raisins or sultanas, a few currants, a little mixed peel, syrup and a sprinkling of mixed spice. Roll up and seal edges. Dip a pudding cloth into boiling water and dredge it with flour. Wrap the pudding in this and tie the ends. Put into boiling water and boil 2½ hours.

PUMPKIN PIE

Short pastry.
1½ lbs. pumpkin.
Sugar to taste.

2 ozs. sultanas.
1 teaspoonful ground ginger.

Prepare pumpkin, steam till tender, mash with fork, add sugar (brown, if possible), sultanas and ginger.

Line plate with pastry, pile on mixture thickly (an inch deep at least), cover with pastry, bake about 30 minutes.

RAISIN AND SAGO PUDDING

¼ lb. sago or tapioca.
1 breakfastcupful bread-crumbs.
1 breakfastcupful stoned raisins.
1 oz. chopped suet.

2 ozs. sugar.
1 teaspoonful bicarbonate of soda.
1 cupful milk and water in equal parts.

Soak sago or tapioca in milk and water for an hour or so, then mix with breadcrumbs, raisins, suet, sugar, and bicarbonate of soda dissolved in a little warm milk. Stir well, turn into greased basin and steam for 2 hours.

RHUBARB SPONGE

1 lb. rhubarb.
6 ozs. flour.
3 ozs. margarine.
4 ozs. sugar.

1 egg or equivalent in egg substitute.
Ginger to taste.

Cut rhubarb in short lengths and put in pie dish with 2 ozs. sugar and ginger.

Beat margarine and remaining sugar to a cream, add egg well beaten. Add flour gradually, mixing well. If egg substitute is used, add it to flour ; proceed as before, substituting a little milk for beaten egg.

Pour mixture over rhubarb. Bake in moderate oven 45–50 minutes till browned and firm.

Windsor Castle

There'll always be an England

LAND OF TRADITION ..

...WHERE

HUNTLEY & PALMERS

BISCUITS

will always be pre-eminent

SHROVE TUESDAY PANCAKES

1 tablespoonful custard powder.

3 tablespoonfuls self-raising flour.

Pinch of salt.

1 teaspoonful salad oil.

About ½ pint milk.

Few drops lemon flavouring (optional.)

Mix dry ingredients and lemon flavouring tógether. Make well in centre, pour in a little milk, gradually stir in flour, adding up to half the milk. Beat for five minutes. Stir in more milk to make a smooth batter of the usual consistency. Add oil. Beat for a minute. Let batter stand one hour or longer. Fry in lard or cooking fat. These pancakes are as light as if made with eggs.

STEAMED RICE AND APPLE PUDDING

6 ozs. rice.

5 or 6 medium-sized apples

3 dessertspoonfuls sugar.

3 or 4 cloves or a little cinnamon or ground ginger, pinch of salt.

Cook rice with a pinch of salt in a little water till tender. Strain in colander. Pare and core apples, cut in slices, add to rice with sugar and cloves or spice. Do not over-spice, for the flavour of the apple permeates the rice. Mix ingredients well together, and pack into greased pudding basin. Cover with greaseproof paper and tie down. Room must be left for the rice to swell as it absorbs the juice of the apples. Steam for 1½ to 2 hours.

Turn out carefully and serve with golden syrup, or a simple sauce.

STICKY APPLE CHARLOTTE

1 lb. apples.

3 ozs. sugar (brown, if possible).

2 ozs. margarine.

Stale bread.

Nutmeg or clove to flavour.

Grease pie dish and dust with sugar, line with thin slices of bread spread with margarine. Stew the apples to a pulp in very little water with sugar, flavour to taste with clove or nutmeg. Fill prepared pie dish with apple pulp and cover with thin slices of bread and margarine, having margarine on the outside of the slices. Sprinkle with sugar. Bake in hot oven till golden brown.

SUMMER PUDDING

Juicy soft fruit (about 1 lb.), raspberries, loganberries or strawberries.	Slices of stale bread. Sugar to sweeten.

Stew fruit with sugar to taste, and, if necessary, a little water to prevent burning, until tender but not mushy. Line a greased basin or mould with slices of bread, pour in fruit to half fill it, put in a layer of bread to fit the basin, and fill up with the rest of the fruit. Cover with more bread, press down contents of mould, and put on top a weighted plate to keep pudding firm. Leave in cool place till next day, turn out mould, serve very cold with a custard sauce.

If fruit is preferred uncooked, sprinkle over 2–3 ozs. sugar and leave 1 hour to draw juice before putting in the mould. The secret of success of this pudding is to press out the juice into the bread so that it is thoroughly saturated. Stale cake can be used in place of bread.

TAPIOCA FLUFF

$\frac{3}{4}$ oz. tapioca	1 tablespoonful sugar.
$\frac{1}{2}$ pint milk	Vanilla or other flavouring
1 egg	

Bring milk to boil, sprinkle into it the tapioca. Cook gently about $\frac{1}{2}$ an hour till the grains are quite clear. Then add sugar. Cool a little, add beaten yolk of egg. Stir well. Lastly, add flavouring and fold in stiffly beaten white of egg. Pour into a dish and serve.

CHAPTER XI

CAKES, "COOKIES" AND BISCUITS

THERE are fashions in cakes. Apart even from the necessity for more economical use of fat, eggs and sugar, plainer cakes are now preferred. Old recipes are often far much sweeter cakes than those appealing to modern taste. Plain fruit or spice cakes, made with margarine or dripping, no eggs or very few, and half the quantity of sugar usually recommended, together with small "cookies", buns and both sweet and plain biscuits meet the requirements of today.

A revival of the country-house fashion for serving slices or fingers of simple cakes—fruit, seed, ginger—with fresh or stewed fruit at luncheon has become general. Another country idea now regarded with favour by town housewives is fresh or dried fruit "cake" with top and bottom layer of pastry and a fruit filling, cut into squares or fingers.

APPLE CAKE

Pastry.	1 oz. margarine.
1 lb. apples.	Powdered cloves or cinna-
2 tablespoonfuls sugar	mon.

Make a thick puree of apples stewed gently with sugar, margarine and spice, and a very little water. Beat well together when apples are cooked.

Line oblong or square tin with pastry. Spread with puree and cover over with thin layer of pastry. Make small incision in centre to allow steam to escape. Bake in good oven till light golden brown. Sprinkle over with castor sugar while still hot. Cut into squares. This can be eaten at lunch or tea and is good hot or cold. Any left over can be reheated.

BANBURY CAKES

4 ozs. mixed fruits (currants and raisins or sultanas).
1 oz. candied mixed peel.

1 oz. sugar.
1 white of egg.
¾ lb. flaky pastry.

Chop or mince fruit, stoning raisins. Beat white of egg and use part for mixing filling.

Roll out pastry, cut into diamond shapes. Spread with filling. Damp round edges and cover with pastry. Make cut in top of each cake and glaze with remainder of beaten white of egg. Edges must be pinched together and tops dusted over with sugar. Bake in hot oven.

CUT-AND-COME-AGAIN EGGLESS CAKE

8 ozs. flour.
2 ozs. sugar.
2 ozs. margarine or lard.
3 ozs. currants.
1 level teaspoonful bicarbonate of soda.

1 level teaspoonful spice.
Pinch of salt.
½ pint milk.
1 tablespoonful vinegar.

Sieve flour with salt, bicarbonate of soda and spice, rub in fat. Add sugar and currants, stir in the milk gradually. When milk is well beaten in, add vinegar, little by little, to prevent curdling. Bake in greased tin in moderate oven 1 hour.

GINGER SPONGE CAKE

1 cupful flour.
2 ozs. margarine.
2 tablespoonfuls syrup.
1 tablespoonful sugar.
¾ teaspoonful bicarbonate of soda

¾ teaspoonful ground ginger.
A little milk.
1 tablespoonful hot water.

Add ginger to flour, sieve. Melt together margarine, sugar and syrup in saucepan, and mix into flour.

Dissolve bicarbonate of soda in milk, add to other ingredients, and mix well in. Beat well, and stir in water last of all. Pour mixture into greased, shallow tin, and bake in moderate oven for about 30 minutes.

With the ginger a little allspice, grated nutmeg or cinnamon may be added to the flour, if desired.

GOOD FRIDAY SPICED BUNS

1 lb. flour.
2 ozs. margarine or lard.
1½ oz. sugar.
1 teaspoonful spice
1 oz. yeast.
1 teaspoonful salt.

2 ozs. currants.
A little candied peel, if available.
½ pint milk or milk and water.

Mix together sieved flour, salt and spice. Rub in the fat, add currants and peel. Cream yeast and sugar together and add the milk warmed. Mix into dry ingredients, making a soft dough ; leave in a warm place to rise till double its size. When risen, knead on floured board, form into rounds, flatten each and mark deeply with a cross with the back of a knife. Leave to rise again for about 20 minutes. Bake in hot oven 20 minutes.

HONEY CAKES

6 ozs. flour.
2 ozs. margarine.
2 ozs. sugar.
1 egg or equivalent in egg substitute.

½ teacupful honey.
¼ teaspoonful bicarbonate of soda

Beat margarine and sugar to a cream, add honey and egg. Then flour and bicarbonate of soda well mixed ; if egg substitute is used, mix with flour and bicarbonate of soda before adding. Mix all thoroughly. Drop in spoonfuls on greased baking tin. Bake in moderate oven 10 to 15 minutes.

KENTISH TEA CAKES

¼ lb. flour.	1 oz. sugar.
2 ozs. lard.	Pinch of salt, water
2 ozs. currants or sultanas.	Lard for frying
½ teaspoonful baking powder.	

Mix dry ingredients well together, rub lard in and add currants. Mix with sufficient water to make a light dough. Roll out, and form into small round cakes. Fry in lard.

PARKIN

½ lb. flour.	2 teaspoonfuls ground ginger.
½ lb. oatmeal.	½ teaspoonful bicarbonate of soda.
2 ozs. lard.	
2 ozs. margarine.	
2 tablespoonfuls brown sugar.	Pinch of salt.
½ lb. syrup	About ¼ pint milk.

Rub fat into all dry ingredients, except bicarbonate of soda. Slightly warm syrup with a little of the milk and add to other ingredients. Then add bicarbonate of soda dissolved in rest of the milk. Mixture should be smooth, but not drop too easily from a spoon. Add a little more milk if necessary.

Grease a Yorkshire pudding tin and pour in mixture. Bake in very moderate oven about 1–1¼ hours. When cooked, cut into squares.

POTATO GIRDLE CAKES

¼ lb. cooked sieved potato	1 teaspoonful bicarbonate of soda.
¼ lb. flour.	
About ½ pint milk or milk and water.	½ teaspoonful cream of tartar.
	Pinch of salt.

Add salt and rising agents to flour, gradually stir in potato and liquid, using a little more liquid if necessary

—mixture should be thin enough to pour in small quantities on to a greased frying-pan or girdle. Cook for a few minutes each side until lightly browned.

SEED CAKE

Seed cake, both rich and plain, was one of the great institutions in old-time English hospitality. This recipe supplies what is required nowadays—a cake of general utility suitable for the eleven-in-the-morning snack that early risers need, or for teatime.

1 lb. flour.	1 small teaspoonful mixed spice.
5 ozs. margarine or well clarified dripping.	1 teaspoonful bicarbonate of soda.
4 ozs. sugar.	1 teaspoonful vinegar
1 tablespoonful caraway seeds.	$\frac{1}{2}$ pint milk.
	Pinch of salt.

Rub fat into sieved flour into which salt, spice and seeds have been mixed. Add sugar and mix altogether thoroughly. Dissolve soda in warmed milk, add vinegar and stir into cake mixture. Beat well together. Bake in greased tin in moderate oven $1\frac{1}{4}$ hours.

SOUR MILK FRUIT CAKE

1 lb. flour.	$\frac{1}{4}$ lb. fat (margarine is best).
1 teaspoonful bicarbonate of soda.	8 ozs. mixed fruit.
$\frac{1}{4}$ lb. sugar.	$\frac{1}{2}$ nutmeg, grated.
	$\frac{1}{2}$ pint sour milk

Sift flour and soda, rub in margarine, add sugar and fruit and grated nutmeg. Mix well with sour milk to a dropping consistency. Bake for 1 hour in moderate oven.

When turned out this cake should be very brown, like Christmas cake. It can be kept fresh for weeks in an airtight tin.

SLY CAKE

County Durham has a sly cake which meets present-day need for a simple delicacy suitable for teatime or luncheon sweet.

For Pastry

½ lb. self-raising flour.   Pinch of salt.
¼ lb. margarine and lard
mixed.

For Filling

4 ozs. currants.   A medium-sized apple thin-
½ oz. margarine.   ly sliced may be added,
1 oz. sugar,   in which case use fewer
Spice as liked   currants, but more sugar.

Roll out rather more than half the pastry into oblong or square shape. Spread filling, well mixed together, evenly over. Trim edges, cover with remainder of pastry rolled out thinly, press edges together. Score over top in trellised design. Brush lightly over with beaten white of egg or with water and sprinkle with a little castor sugar. Cook in good oven till pale brown, about ½ hour. Cut sly cake into squares.

TREACLE SCONES

½ lb. flour.   2 teaspoonfuls baking pow-
2 tablespoonfuls treacle   der.
1 oz. dripping or lard.   Pinch of salt.
                                     Milk.

Mix together all dry ingredients. Rub in fat. Warm treacle, mix with a little milk, add to mixture. Add more milk to make fairly soft dough. Turn dough on to floured board, knead till smooth, roll into circular form. Bake in oven 10–15 minutes and cut into triangles when nearly cold.

VANILLA CHOCOLATE CAKE

¾ lb. flour.
3 ozs. margarine.
2 heaped tablespoonfuls cocoa powder.
2 tablespoonfuls golden syrup.

2 ozs. sugar.
1 teaspoonful bicarbonate of soda.
¼ pint milk.
Few drops vanilla essence.

Rub margarine into sieved flour, add sugar, cocoa powder, slightly warmed milk in which soda has been dissolved, flavouring, and last of all the golden syrup warmed a little. Beat all well together, bake for 1¼ hours in round tin lined with greaseproof paper.

WARTIME SANDWICH

¼ lb. self-raising flour.
1 teaspoonful egg substitute.

3 ozs. sugar.
About 1 gill milk.
Pinch of salt.

Mix dry ingredients in basin. Add milk by degrees, and beat 10 minutes ; mixture should not be too thin. Bake in two greased sandwich tins in hot oven 20 minutes. Remove. Turn on to cake rack. Leave till cold. Spread with jam.

WHOLEMEAL SCONES

1 lb. wholemeal flour.
2 teaspoonfuls baking powder.

Pinch of salt.
1 egg well-beaten in a little milk.

Mix together dry ingredients and make into a soft dough with the egg and milk, using more milk if necessary. Roll out on floured board, cut into rounds or triangles. Bake in hot oven 10 minutes.

YULE LOAF

2½ lbs. flour.
8 ozs. cooking fat (half should be lard).
½ lb. sugar.
1 lb. mixed fruit (half should be raisins).
2 ozs. yeast

1 tablespoonful finely shredded candied peel (optional).
1 teaspoonful mixed spice.
Nutmeg to taste
1 egg.
Pinch of salt.
Warm water.

Dissolve yeast with 1 teaspoonful of the sugar in

How to use

EIFFEL TOWER LEMONADE CRYSTALS

For all culinary purposes

Wherever you would use the juice of one lemon, use two medium-sized heaped teaspoons of Eiffel Tower Lemonade Crystals dissolved in two tablespoons of hot or cold water.

FOR FLAVOURING FISH AND PANCAKES
Dissolve crystals as above, put into a sprinkling bottle and sprinkle over as desired.

FOR BUNS, CAKES, PUDDINGS, STEWED APPLES and
for all other purposes for which lemon is desired, dissolve the required quantity of Lemonade Crystals and mix with the other ingredients.

The following recipes are recommended

LEMON CURD

Foster Clark's Cream Custard Powder	Contents of a 1 pint bag
Eiffel Tower Lemonade Crystals	2 medium-sized heaped teaspoons
Sugar	2 oz.
Margarine	1 level teaspoonful
Bicarbonate of Soda	1 level saltspoonful
Water	½ pint and 1 tablespoonful

Put the powder and crystals into a basin and mix into a smooth paste with the tablespoonful of water. Boil the ½ pint of water with the sugar in a saucepan and when boiling pour on to the paste in the basin and stir well.

Return to the saucepan, stir in the margarine and boil up. The lemon curd will then be ready for use.

LEMON CURD TARTLETS

Flour	½ lb.
Baking Powder	1 teaspoonful
Margarine	¼ oz.
Pinch of Salt	
Cold Water	

Sift the flour, baking powder, and salt into a basin. Rub in the margarine to the consistency of breadcrumbs. Mix with the water to a stiffish paste, using only enough water to hold the ingredients together.

Roll out thin on a slightly floured board, and line patty tins. Prick the pastry shells well with a fork so that the shells will not blister while baking.

Bake (without filling) in a quick oven. When baked remove the shells and fill with lemon curd.

This is sufficient to make 18 tartlets.

LEMON TRIFLE

4 Sponge Cakes	
Eiffel Tower Lemonade Crystals	2 medium-heaped teaspoons
Cold Water	½ teacupful (about 4 oz.)
Sugar	1 tablespoon (1 oz.)
Custard Sauce	½ pint

Place the sponge cakes in a glass dish.

Dissolve the lemonade crystals and sugar in the water and sprinkle it evenly over the sponge cakes.

Prepare ½ pint of custard sauce, using Foster Clark's vanilla cream custard powder, and pour it over the sponge cakes.

Set aside and serve when cold.

The trifle may be decorated with blanched almonds, ratafia biscuits or fruit

LEMON SAUCE FOR USE WITH FISH
OR BOILED FOWL

Flour	1 tablespoonful
Margarine	1 oz.
Milk	½ pint
Salt	A saltspoonful
Eiffel Tower Lemonade Crystals	1 medium-heaped teaspoonful
Water	1 tablespoonful

Melt the fat, add the flour, cook for 2 minutes. Add the salt and milk; bring to boiling point and simmer gently for another 2 minutes. Remove saucepan from heat. Dissolve the lemonade crystals in the water and pour into the sauce in the pan, stirring well.

Before serving, make the sauce hot, but do not boil.

a cupful of warm water. Add salt to sieved flour, rub in fat, mix in fruit, peel, if used, sugar and spices. Make well in centre of flour, pour in yeast, and let it rise for 15 minutes. Stir in well-beaten egg to make a dough, adding a little more warm water if necessary. Leave this dough to rise about 1 hour. Knead well, form into loaves and put into greased tins, either round or bread loaf shape. Let loaves rise again, then bake in hot oven, reducing heat later. Time varies according to size of loaves.

Yule loaf is cut into slices and buttered when required.

YULETIDE FRUIT CAKE

10 ozs. self-raising flour	1 dessertspoonful vinegar.
$\frac{1}{4}$ lb. margarine.	1 tablespoonful golden syrup
$\frac{1}{4}$ lb. chopped raisins, dates. or other dried fruit.	or treacle. Egg substitute (equivalent of one egg).
3 ozs. sugar.	
$\frac{1}{4}$ pint milk.	$\frac{1}{2}$ teaspoonful mixed spice.
1 teaspoonful bicarbonate of soda.	

Rub sieved flour with margarine. Add all dry ingredients. Dissolve bicarbonate of soda in slightly warmed milk. Stir into mixture, then add syrup slightly warmed. Lastly, vinegar. Bake in hot oven $\frac{1}{4}$ hour. Reduce heat and bake 1 hour longer. This cake looks dark and rich.

To Fill Biscuit Tin

CANADIAN GINGER COOKIES

$\frac{1}{2}$ teacupful treacle or syrup.	1 teaspoonful bicarbonate of soda.
1 oz. margarine or dripping.	$\frac{1}{2}$ teacupful hot water Flour.
1 teaspoonful ground ginger.	

Warm syrup with fat in basin, add ground ginger,

and bicarbonate of soda dissolved in hot water. Add enough flour to make the mixture a pliable dough. Roll out, cut into rounds, and bake in quick oven about 20 minutes.

CHOCOLATE BISCUITS

1 oz. cocoa powder.	¼ teaspoonful bicarbonate of soda.
4 ozs. flour.	
2 ozs. sugar.	1 tablespoonful syrup.
2 ozs. margarine.	

Sieve dry ingredients. Melt the margarine and syrup a little, and mix all together thoroughly. Beat well, roll out and cut into shapes. Bake for about 15 minutes.

Vanilla essence or other flavouring may be used.

DUTCH COOKIES

1¼ teacupfuls flour	1 oz. blanched, chopped nuts.
½ teacupful sugar.	
2 ozs. cooking fat	Pinch salt.

Mix dry ingredients together, and rub in the fat. Work with fingertips until thoroughly kneaded, adding nuts last. Roll out thinly, cut into rounds, and bake in oven until crisp, about 20 minutes.

JUMBLES

Jumbles may be kept in rounds, or after they leave the oven, rolled round a stick. This is an eggless recipe.

¼ lb. flour.	2 ozs. sugar.
¼ lb. margarine.	1 teaspoonful powdered ginger.
¼ lb. syrup.	

Cream margarine, add sugar and syrup, mixing well together. Add sieved flour, to which ginger has been added.

Drop spoonfuls of mixture in circles on to a greased tin, and bake in medium oven till the jumbles are a golden brown.

OATCAKES

½ lb. medium oatmeal.
2 ozs. fat.
Pinch bicarbonate of soda.

Pinch of salt.
Hot water for mixing

Mix dry ingredients together. Mix fat with a little hot water, add gradually to dry ingredients to make a pliable dough. Knead, and roll out thinly on a board well covered with oatmeal. Cut in rounds, bake in moderate oven about 30 minutes.

SWEET OATMEAL BISCUITS

¼ lb. oatmeal, medium or fine.
¼ lb. flour.
2 ozs. margarine.

2 ozs. sugar.
1 teaspoonful baking pow-der.
Milk to mix

Mix dry ingredients, rub in margarine, and mix to a stiff paste with milk. Roll out thinly, cut in rounds, and bake a light brown.

WINE BISCUITS

1 lb. flour.
¼ lb. margarine.
2 tablespoonfuls castor sugar.
1 egg.
A little milk.

Cinnamon, ginger, or carra-way for flavouring, about 1½ teaspoonfuls.
Almond or other essence to taste

Rub fat into sieved flour, add sugar and flavouring, and stir in well-beaten egg. Add sufficient milk to make a fairly stiff paste which can be rolled thinly on a floured board. Cut into shapes with fancy cutter and bake in moderate oven 10 minutes. If stored in airtight tin, these biscuits keep for some time.

CHAPTER XII

WHEN THE CAN IS OPENED

HOUSEWIVES are converted to the use of canned foods of every variety, and the enterprise of British canning firms has added greatly to the choice of vegetables, soups, fish, complete meat dishes for reheating, savoury rolls, galantines and other aids to housekeeping. They have learned too that these viands make attractive meals when combined with fresh vegetables, cereals and salads. A small tin of oxtail soup, for instance, gives meaty appearance and taste to a stew or casserole of home-grown root vegetables.

Canned foods are packed at the moment when they are at their best. Once the can is opened, however, it is advisable that the contents should be used quickly. Cooks should decide on a plan, therefore, before they open a tin.

TIN OF TOMATO JUICE:

(1) Tomato soup, by adding 2 tablespoonfuls juice to ½ pint milk and water or vegetable stock, thickening with 1 teaspoonful cornflour, and seasoning.

(2) Tomato sauce to accompany fish or meat, by adding 1 tablespoonful of juice to a gill of plain white sauce.

(3) There will still be sufficient in a small can to flavour a stew or hot-pot, or, if preferred, to serve with a dash of Worcester sauce as non-alcoholic cocktail.

TIN OF PEAS:

(1) Vegetable course, or accompaniments.
(2) Garnish for a made dish.
(3) Garnish for stew or green pea soup.

Tin of Asparagus:

(1) Hot vegetable, with melted margarine, or cold, with oil and vinegar.

(2) A few points may be reserved for omelette, or as garnish for fish, or as sandwich filling.

(3) Water in which asparagus has been heated provides basis for asparagus cream soup made with milk, thickening, a little fat, seasoning and possibly yolk of egg.

Tin of Celery:

(1) Vegetable dish with white sauce or au gratin.

(2) Hearts may be served as a salad.

(3) Addition to soup, stew or hot-pot.

CELERY AND RICE AU GRATIN

Celery.	Salt and pepper.
2 ozs. rice.	Nutmeg.
½ pint white sauce.	Grated cheese.

Drain celery, cut in small pieces. Cook rice. Have ready white sauce in pan, into it put the celery and rice, seasoning, a pinch of nutmeg and a little grated cheese. Simmer gently 15 minutes.

MEAT ROLL RAGOUT

1 tin meat roll or corned beef.	1½ ozs. flour.
Cold cooked potatoes.	1 tablespoonful tomato ketchup.
2 carrots, 1 turnip, 2 onions.	1 pint water.
1½ ozs. dripping.	Salt and pepper.

Melt dripping in saucepan, add onion coarsely chopped, carrot and turnip cut in dice. Fry till lightly browned. Sprinkle in flour, stir and cook slowly till brown. Add water, stirring to remove lumps, add seasoning. Simmer slowly 30 minutes, add tomato ketchup, meat and potatoes cut into cubes. Simmer very slowly till meat and potatoes are heated through:

SALMON SOUFFLE

1 tin salmon.	Margarine.
½ pint white sauce.	Seasoning.
1 egg.	Browned breadcrumbs.
1 dessertspoonful parsley.	

The charm of this dish is its creamy, light texture. It makes a good main dish. Flake contents of a tin of salmon, after draining, into a basin. Add yolk of egg, mix well. Stir in white sauce (not too thick), also chopped parsley. Beat up white of egg stiffly, fold into salmon. Put into greased fireproof dish, sprinkle with browned breadcrumbs and little dabs of margarine. Bake 20–30 minutes.

SCALLOPED LOBSTER

1 tin lobster or crab.	Margarine.
⅛ pint white sauce.	Browned breadcrumbs.
½ teaspoonful anchovy essence.	Grated cheese.
	Salt, pepper, cayenne.

Drain lobster or crab and chop in small pieces. Put into a saucepan with the white sauce, anchovy essence, seasonings. Mix well, make thoroughly hot. Grease scallop shells or fireproof dish, nearly fill with fish and sauce. Cover the surface with browned breadcrumbs, sprinkle lightly with cheese, lay on top a few small pieces of margarine. Bake in quick oven 15–20 minutes.

VEGETABLE PATTIES

1 tin mixed vegetables.	Rough puff pastry.
⅛ pint thick white sauce.	Salt and pepper.

Roll out paste to ½ inch thickness. Stamp out rounds with a 2-inch pastry cutter. With a smaller cutter stamp half through the pastry. Bake in hot oven 20 minutes. When cooked take out centre piece with a pointed knife. Remove the soft centre, fill with the following hot mixture.

Drain vegetables. Put them with white sauce in a saucepan with seasoning. Make thoroughly hot and fill pastry cases. After filling, patties should be returned to the oven, and served when really hot.

CANNED FOOD CALENDAR

Variety	*Period of Keeping*
Meat and fish	Indefinitely. Keep in cool, dry place. Fish packed in oil improves with storing.
Ready-to-serve dishes (meat and vegetables)	2 to 3 years.
Soups	Indefinitely.
Vegetables	Up to 3 years.
Fruit	1 year.
Ready-to-serve puddings	At least 1 year.
Tinned milk :	
Sweetened	Up to 6 months, not more than 9 months.
Unsweetened ..	From 2 to 3 years.

PART II

STOCKING THE STORE CUPBOARD

THE new economy is filling up the store cupboards of the home which have not been so well stocked with home-preserved and bottled vegetables and fruits within living memory. Store sauces, ketchups, pickles and salad creams are other additions. Methods which can be carried out successfully without outlay on costly equipment are detailed here with a selection of simple recipes.

The variety that is so desirable can be secured by a system of friendly exchange. A housewife who has a superfluity of some form of preserve can barter with a neighbour for something of which she may have more than she requires. In this manner splendid reserve supplies are built up without wastage or unnecessary expense.

Label all preserves with their name and date and make an inventory of store-cupboard contents. It is a good plan to post this up inside store cupboard door and enter up dates of withdrawals for use.

CHAPTER I

JAMS, JELLIES AND CHEESES

APPLE GINGER

Apple Ginger is a good breakfast preserve. It also makes a filling for sandwiches.

2 lbs. cooking apples.
1 tumblerful water.
1½ lbs. sugar.
½ teaspoonful lemon substitute or citric acid.

Pinch of cayenne.
1 oz. whole ginger or 2 ozs. chopped preserved ginger, or 1 teaspoonful ground ginger.

Prepare apples, peeling, coring and chopping them. Cook in water with ginger (bruised and tied in muslin if whole ginger), lemon substitute and cayenne till apples are tender. Add sugar. Simmer till sugar dissolves. Boil rapidly till preserve sets when tested.

BITTER ORANGE MARMALADE

The attraction of this recipe is the quantity produced.

8 bitter oranges.
8 lbs. sugar.

8 pints water.

Wash oranges and slice thinly. Cover with the water, keeping back ½ pint, and leave to soak 24 hours. Remove pips from oranges, put into a separate basin, just cover with remaining ½ pint water, and soak same time as oranges. Then put sliced oranges and water into preserving pan. Tie pips in muslin bag and add them and water in which they soaked to pan, boil slowly 1½

hours. Add sugar (warmed) and heat gently till sugar has dissolved, then bring to boil and boil rapidly for 20–30 minutes till marmalade sets when tested.

CHERRY CHEESE

1 lb. cherries (sweet or cooking variety). ½ lb. sugar.

Put cherries in pan, add a little water to prevent burning. Cover closely and simmer gently till perfectly soft. Pass through a sieve, return to pan, add sugar, boil for ¾–1 hour, stirring constantly till it is of a very thick consistency—like jelly. Turn into small jars.

A useful filling for cakes, or can be used as a sweet with slices of sponge cake.

DAMSON CHEESE

A useful fruit filling for cakes, accompaniment to sweet or can be served with meat in place of red-currant jelly.

2 lbs. damsons. ½ lb. sugar.

Put damsons, stalked, in earthenware jar or basin, cover and place in a saucepan of water. Bring to boil and allow fruit to boil in its own rich juice till nearly dry, when stones are removed and sugar is added. Mix sugar well with fruit, simmer slowly 2 hours. Finally let it boil rapidly ½ hour.

ECONOMICAL MINCEMEAT

1 lb. chopped apples.
¾ lb. currants.
½ lb. raisins.
½ lb. sultanas.
2 ozs. chopped candied peel.
½ lb. beef suet.
½ lb. light brown or castor sugar.

½ teaspoonful lemon substitute.
¼ teaspoonful ground mace.
¼ teaspoonful ground cinnamon.
⅛ teaspoonful mixed spice.

Chop the suet. Add apples peeled and cored, chopped and stoned raisins, sultanas, currants and mixed peel.

Mix well, stir in spices, sugar and lemon substitute. Pack tightly into jars. Cover closely and keep in a cool dry place.

ANOTHER METHOD :—

½ lb. apples.	½ lb. sugar.
½ lb. sultanas.	¼ lb. margarine.
½ lb. currants.	1 teaspoonful nutmeg or mixed spice.
¼ lb. raisins.	
2 ozs. mixed peel.	½ teaspoonful salt.
2 ozs. almonds or other nuts.	½ teaspoonful lemon substitute.

Clean fruit, chop apples and raisins, grate nuts. Mix dry ingredients, add margarine melted and lemon substitute. Pack tightly into jars and tie down.

FRESH FRUIT RASPBERRY JAM

This is an economical jam and preserves the flavour of the fresh fruit. It keeps well.

Equal quantities of raspberries and sugar.

Put raspberries in preserving pan, crush them with a wooden spoon. Heat them and stir till they nearly boil.

Meanwhile heat sugar in oven and add to raspberries. Bring contents of pan to boil, remove as soon as boiling. Pot and cover while hot.

MINT JELLY

4 ozs. mint leaves.	1 oz. powdered gelatine.
½ lb. loaf sugar.	¾ pint water.
¼ pint white vinegar.	

Strip mint leaves from stalks, chop them finely. Dissolve sugar in vinegar, add ½ pint of the water, then add the chopped mint and simmer for 10 minutes. Put the gelatine in ¼ pint hot water, stirring till it dissolves, then add to the vinegar and mint. When slightly cool, strain and pot.

ORANGE RIND MARMALADE

Rind of 2 oranges (3 ozs.).   1 lb. sugar.
1 lb. cooking apples.

Shred rind, soak in ½ pint water 2 days. Cut apples in pieces (do not peel or core), put in pan with water to cover. Simmer till soft, strain through cloth till 1 pint juice is obtained.

Put rind, water and apple juice in pan. Simmer till rind is tender and contents of pan measure 1 pint. Add sugar, let it dissolve. Bring to boil and boil rapidly till marmalade sets when tested, 15 to 20 minutes. (An officially recommended recipe.)

RHUBARB JAM

This preserve is for immediate use, its advantage being that it takes very little sugar.

1 lb. rhubarb.   ½ teaspoonful ground gin-
4 ozs. sugar.   ger.

Cut up rhubarb in small pieces, place in saucepan with just enough water to prevent burning, add sugar and ground ginger. Bring to boil, boil briskly 15 to 20 minutes. Pot. There is no necessity to test for setting or to cover in usual way as this jam will not keep.

To make a keeping jam, use ¾ lb. sugar to 1 lb. rhubarb, then proceed as above.

ROWAN JELLY

Equal quantities of sliced   1 lb. sugar to 1 pint juice.
   apples and rowan ber-
   ries.

Cut up but do not peel apples. Stalk and wash berries. Put all into preserving pan with very little water, just enough to prevent burning. Cook slowly till a pulp, strain through muslin, letting liquid drop into bowl. Measure and put into preserving pan with sugar. Boil till it sets, about ¾ hour.

SEEDLESS BLACKBERRY JAM

3 lbs. blackberries   3½ lbs. sugar
1½ lbs. apples.

Put blackberries in preserving pan, adding just over a gill of water. Boil till juice is fully extracted. Strain through hair sieve. Peel and core apples and cook them in the blackberry juice till tender. Add sugar, boil and test to see that it will "jell".

WHOLE FRUIT PLUM JAM

1 lb. red or yellow plums   If unripe, allow a little
(fairly ripe).   more sugar
¾ lb. sugar.

Weigh and wash plums. Cut up, stone carefully and place in a large dish, with alternate layers of sugar and fruit. Leave in cool place overnight. Turn into preserving pan and bring slowly to boil, boil rapidly 30–35 minutes, stirring frequently.

CHAPTER II

BOTTLING SUMMER FRUITS

WOMEN today find, as their grandmothers did, that a shelf stocked with jars of home bottled fruits is an asset to winter catering. The novice will succeed at the simple processes of fruit bottling provided she carries out instructions with care and intelligence.

D

For sterilisation by immersion in boiling water she can use either screw-band bottles, jam jars with special closures (these closures are suitable for the boiling method only) or jam jars covered with a synthetic skin.

For oven sterilisation use either screw-band bottles or jam jars, but the latter must be sealed afterwards.

When screw-band jars are used, be sure glass is not chipped round top or there will not be a good vacuum. Always use new rubber rings.

Now for the fruit. This must be sound, ripe but firm, cleaned, dried and packed tightly in bottles. Next comes the sugar question. Fill up bottles of fruit either with water or a syrup. Advantage of syrup is that the fruit retains colour and flavour and that only half the sugar is required when fruit is used.

WITHOUT SUGAR

Use round-necked jam jars. Warm jars in oven, pack with fruit, place in oven with very low heat, warm gradually. In an hour fruit should have shrunk.

Take out one jar at a time, fill to within $\frac{1}{2}$ inch of top with boiling water. Seal immediately by covering jar with three thicknesses of greaseproof paper, each pasted down with a flour and water paste. Take out next jar, repeat process.

If screw-top bottles are used for this method, pack with fruit, put on rubber rings, lids and screw-bands but do not screw tight as steam must escape. Follow above procedure. When sterilisation is completed, take out bottles one by one, tighten screw-band immediately, wait for bottles to get cold, then test seal by removing screw-bands and seeing if lid remains firm. If it comes off, re-sterilisation is necessary. Fault may be due to chipped jar ; examine top of jar, and, if chipped, put fruit in new jar. Renew rubber ring, re-sterilise by adding water to within ½ inch of top, heat in oven as before but allow 5 minutes extra.

BOTTLING IN SYRUP

You may use as little as ¼ lb. sugar to 1 pint water but ½ lb. sugar to 1 pint water gives better results. Dissolve sugar in water, bring to boil. Follow same process of bottling as before, pouring syrup over fruit in the same way as water.

WATER STERILISATION

A less popular method is sterilisation in boiling water. It necessitates the use of a thermometer. In this case water or syrup is poured over fruit before heating.

Fill a large saucepan or other vessel with cold water. Pack bottles with fruit, fill up with syrup or water, fit on lids, clips or screw-bands, but in the case of screw-bands screw on and then unscrew half a turn. Arrange a false bottom in saucepan with slats of wood or wire rack, place bottles on it. See that water in pan covers jars, bring it slowly to a temperature of 165°F., taking 1½ hours to do so. Test with thermometer and keep water at that temperature for 15 to 20 minutes. This temperature is right for most fruits except red and black currants, for which it should be 180°F., and for cherries, pears and tomatoes 190°F. Take out bottles quickly, tighten screw-bands immediately ; when cooler, tighten again.

If bottling tomatoes, add ½ oz. salt to each quart of boiling water with which fruit is covered.

PULPING

A useful method of preserving fruit to be made later on into jam or used as a filling for tarts or as an accompaniment to milk pudding.

Put screw-top bottles or jam jars with closures into oven and make them hot. Meanwhile place fruit in saucepan with just sufficient water or syrup to prevent burning. Stew till cooked. Pour while still boiling into hot bottles. Seal immediately.

*　　*　　*　　*　　*

DRIED APPLE RINGS

Apples must be carefully peeled and cored, with all blemishes removed, and cut into rings not more than $\frac{1}{4}$ inch in thickness. The rings should be arranged in single layers on drying trays (made by nailing together four wooden laths, and stretching wire gauze or cheese-cloth across the framework) or threaded on sticks, which can be laid across the trays. Place near the kitchen fire or in a cool oven at a temperature of not more than 140°F.

If the process can be a continuous one the rings should be dry in from 4–6 hours. If the rings are dried at the end of the day when the stove heat is dying down, drying may continue intermittently over a period of 2–3 days.

When the fruit is sufficiently dry the texture should resemble that of chamois leather, and if a handful of rings are pressed firmly together the slices should be springy enough to separate at once on being released from the hand. When they have reached this stage they should be removed from the oven and left for 12 hours, then packed and stored in a dry place. (Officially recommended recipe.)

TO PRESERVE BEANS IN SALT

To every 3 or 4 lbs. beans allow 1 lb. salt. Beans must be young, fresh and tender. Do not wash unless necessary. If washed, dry before slicing. Cut them up, if small they may be left whole. Place a good layer of salt in a stoneware jar and on the salt a layer of beans. Continue to fill up jar with alternate layers, pressing beans well down and having top layer of salt. Cover and leave a few days. The beans shrink and the jar may then be filled up with more beans and salt, but take care that the final layer of salt completely covers the beans. Cover jar securely with lid or several layers of paper; if with cork paint over with melted paraffin wax. If the jar is stored in a room with a stone floor, place on a piece of wood.

To use the beans: Remove from salt and soak in 2 or 3 lots of cold water for 12 hours at least. Cook in boiling water till tender. (Officially recommended recipe.)

CHAPTER III

PICKLES AND CHUTNEYS

APPLE CHUTNEY

2¼ lbs. cooking apples.	½ oz. mustard seed.
¾ lb. sultanas.	½ oz. ground ginger.
1 lb. sugar	¼ oz. garlic or a little fine-
1 pint vinegar.	ly chopped onion
1 teaspoonful salt.	Pinch cayenne pepper.

Peel and core apples, and cut up into very small pieces. Cook gently with sugar, ginger and vinegar until apples are tender and reduced to pulp. Add sultanas, spices and other flavourings. Mix thoroughly and let chutney stand in a covered earthenware basin for a few days, stirring from time to time, before bottling in the usual way

BLACKBERRY CHUTNEY

1 lb. blackberries.	1 heaped teaspoonful salt.
½ lb. apples.	¼ teaspoonful mace.
6 ozs. sugar.	½ teaspoonful mustard.
2 onions.	⅛ teaspoonful ginger.
⅛ pint vinegar	

Cook slowly all ingredients, except sugar, for a good hour. Add sugar and resume cooking slowly till of a thick consistency. (If oven is on, and not too hot, this can be done best in fireproof earthenware jar.) Sieve to remove seeds.

ELDERBERRY CHUTNEY

1½ lbs. elderberries.	½ oz. ground ginger, a few
1 onion.	cloves.
2 ozs. stoned raisins or sultanas.	1 teaspoonful salt.
2 ozs. sugar (preferably brown).	¼ teaspoonful pepper and rather less of mace.
½ pint vinegar.	

Stalk elderberries, press through sieve. Chop onion, and raisins finely and boil with berry pulp and other ingredients 10 to 15 minutes.

GREEN GOOSEBERRY CHUTNEY

1 quart green gooseberries.	1 oz. mustard seed.
6 ozs. sugar.	½ oz. turmeric.
½ lb. onions.	1 oz. ground ginger.
½ lb. sultanas.	3 ozs. salt.
1 pint vinegar.	¼ oz. cayenne pepper.

Chop onions, put into pan with gooseberries—topped, tailed and chopped—and other ingredients. The mustard seed should be crushed before adding. Simmer gently for 1 hour, or until of a thick consistency.

The HOME COOK'S
finest stand-by !

A CAN of Batchelor's Peas, Beans or Carrots gives just that appetising "fillip" to a meal which the home-cook finds such a problem in these days of shortages and rationing.

But "Batchelor's" Canned Foods ensure much more than that ; they are a source of valuable vitamins ; they mean added food-value for the meal ; they bring vital energy-building, body-building, strength-sustaining elements priceless alike to the growing and the grown.

Whenever or wherever you open a can of "Batchelor's" you are assured of freshness and quality unquestionable.

That is why you should always specify "Batchelor's."

Issued in the interests of Housewives by the Proprietors of

CANNED PEAS, BEANS AND CARROTS

IMPORTANT Although output is larger then ever, present conditions are causing a greatly increased demand and we ask the indulgence of those experiencing difficulty over supplies

GREEN TOMATO CHUTNEY

2 lbs. green tomatoes.	1 pint vinegar.
2 lbs. apples.	Salt and pepper.
½ lb. onions.	A few chillies.
½ lb. sugar (brown for preference).	1 small teaspoonful ground ginger.

Slice tomatoes, apples and onions, place all ingredients in a pan. Bring to boil, and simmer slowly for about 3 hours on top of stove, or in the oven.

MIXED PICKLES IN MUSTARD SAUCE

Cauliflowers, marrows or cucumbers.	3 pints vinegar.
	2 ozs. dry mustard.
Onions, snall French beans, young carrots,	2 tablespoonfuls flour.
	1 oz. turmeric powder.

First make the piccalilli sauce by mixing flour, mustard and turmeric to a smooth paste with a little vinegar, gradually adding the remainder of the vinegar.

Put cauliflowers, in small flowerets, marrows or cucumbers cut in cubes, onions, beans and carrots in pan, cover with salt. Leave 48 hours, wash and drain, and add vegetables to sauce mixture. Bring gradually to boil, stirring till boiling point is reached. 30 minutes' boiling completes the process. Watch pan carefully, stirring from time to time. Bottle in wide-necked jars.

MOCK MANGO CHUTNEY

1 lb. cooking plums, which may be hard and green.	¼ teaspoonful cayenne pepper.
½ lb. sugar.	½ teaspoonful ground ginger.
¼ lb. dates.	
1 small onion.	A generous ¼ pint vinegar.
½ oz. salt.	

Halve plums, removing stones, and cook gently in vinegar. Strain. In same vinegar cook chopped dates and onion, adding sugar and salt when onions are cooked. Pour over plums, and when syrup is cold, add ginger and cayenne. Mix well and cook slowly in saucepan or earthenware jar till thoroughly blended.

SPICED BLACKBERRIES

3 lbs. blackberries	½ teaspoonful cinnamon.
1 lb. sugar.	⅛ teaspoonful ground cloves.
½ pint vinegar.	

Pick and wash the blackberries. Cook together the vinegar, sugar and spices, adding blackberries just before boiling point is reached. Allow contents of pan to simmer for 15 minutes. Bottle and seal down while very hot.

SPICED DAMSONS

4 lbs. damsons.	¼ oz. whole cloves.
2 lbs. sugar.	½ teaspoonful cinnamon.
1 pint vinegar.	½ teaspoonful root ginger.
¼ oz. allspice.	

Prepare spiced vinegar by bringing vinegar to the boil with spices tied in a bag.

Wash fruit and simmer in spiced vinegar with the sugar. When tender, drain fruit into jars and boil up spiced vinegar until it thickens a little ; pour over fruit while hot.

VEGETABLE MARROW PICKLE

4 lbs. vegetable marrow.	8 small chillies.
6 onions.	4 cloves.
½ lb. sugar (brown, if possible).	Small blade of mace.
1 oz. ground ginger.	½ teaspoonful allspice.
1½ ozs. mustard.	6 peppercorns.
½ oz. curry powder (optional).	1 quart vinegar.

Peel and cut up marrow, removing seeds. Sprinkle well with salt. Let stand all night. Next day drain thoroughly. Put vinegar into saucepan, add onions finely sliced, and all the other ingredients, allspice and mace tied in muslin. Bring slowly to boil, simmer 10 minutes. Add marrow and cook for 15–25 minutes. Do not let pieces break. Put into jars and cover when cold.

CHAPTER IV

SAUCES AND SALAD CREAMS

BOTTLED MINT SAUCE

½ pint vinegar.   ½ lb. sugar
¼ lb. chopped mint

Boil vinegar, pour on to mint. Add sugar and stir with a wooden spoon. Bottle cold. Mint will remain a rich green all through the winter.

COOKED SALAD DRESSING

2 ozs. flour.	1½ gills white vinegar.
2 ozs. margarine.	Few drops tarragon vinegar.
1 egg yolk.	2 teaspoonfuls mustard.
½ pint milk.	Salt, pepper.
¾ gill salad oil.	

Melt margarine in pan, sift in flour, cook gently a minute or two, stirring all the time, then add milk gradually. Bring to the boil ; boil a few minutes, stirring well. Turn into a basin and cover with damp cloth till cold. When cold, stir sauce thoroughly, whisk in yolk of egg, then alternately salad oil and vinegar, adding very little at a time. Mix mustard with a little extra vinegar, salt and pepper, then add to sauce. Whisk thoroughly. If too thick use a little more vinegar, if too thin add oil. Pour into jars, cork well.

A HAMPSHIRE SAUCE

Save the spiced vinegar from pickle jars. When a quart is available, chop up 1 onion, 3 apples, 3 tomatoes. Bring all to boil in the vinegar, simmer till contents of pan are a thin puree. Sieve and bottle.

PIQUANT SALAD DRESSING

1 tablespoonful dry mustard.	½ cupful vinegar.
	2 teaspoonfuls sugar
½ tablespoonful Worcester sauce.	½ teaspoonful salt.
	1 teaspoonful grated onion
⅓ cupful tomato pulp or ketchup.	Dash cayenne pepper.
	1 cupful salad oil.

Mix all ingredients and beat with an egg-beater till thoroughly combined. This dressing will keep for several weeks if placed in a covered container.

PLUM SAUCE

2 lbs. cooking plums.	¼ oz. bruised ginger.
½ lb. sugar.	8 cloves.
1 pint vinegar.	½ teaspoonful cayenne
1 heaped teaspoonful salt.	

Wash and stone plums, put into pan with other ingredients. Boil for 30 minutes. Sieve and bottle.

TOMATO SAUCE

3 lbs. ripe tomatoes.	½ pint vinegar.
¼ lb. onions.	1 bayleaf.
1 clove garlic.	10 peppercorns.
3 ozs. sugar (brown, if possible).	Small piece cinnamon.
	1 blade mace.
1 dessertspoonful salt.	1 teaspoonful allspice.
Pinch cayenne.	¼ teaspoonful celery seed
1 dessertspoonful tarragon vinegar.	

Add spices and salt to vinegar, bring to boil, simmer on very low heat 2 hours with lid on. Strain.

Cut up tomatoes, onion and garlic, cook till reduced to a pulp. Rub through sieve, add sugar, salt, cayenne, tarragon vinegar and strained spiced vinegar. Cook sauce till consistency of thick cream. Pour into bottles and seal at once. If corks are used, they should first be soaked in water.

*   *   *   *

The following salad creams are for immediate use, but any left over will keep for a day or two.

EGGLESS SALAD CREAM

½ teaspoonful castor sugar
1 tablespoonful oil.
2 tablespoonfuls milk.
1 tablespoonful vinegar

½ teaspoonful salt, rather less pepper.
½ teaspoonful made mustard

Mix all dry ingredients together. Then add gradually the oil, milk, and lastly the vinegar.

HORSERADISH SALAD CREAM

½ oz. flour.
¾ oz. margarine.
½ pint milk.
¼ teaspoonful sugar.

1 dessertspoonful shredded horseradish.
1 dessertspoonful vinegar
Pepper, salt.

Melt margarine in small saucepan, stir in flour and sugar, cook slightly. Add milk a little at a time. Stir constantly till boiling, add salt and pepper. Stir in the horseradish, finally the vinegar.

MOCK MAYONNAISE

1 teaspoonful unflavoured custard powder
¼ pint milk.

Vinegar.
Salt, pepper.
½ teaspoonful mustard.

Mix custard powder with a little cold milk, heat remainder of milk and, when boiling, pour on to custard powder in basin. Return to saucepan and bring to boil. Add salt, pepper, mustard, and sufficient vinegar to sharpen flavour.

CHAPTER V

HERB PATCH AND SPICE JARS

THE art of flavouring, an ancient one that is ever changing according to prevailing taste, is one of the great secrets of successful cookery. It is flourishing today when the housewife knows the joy of growing and drying her own herbs and appreciates the decorative addition made to her kitchen by the little pottery containers that have replaced the prosaic spice tin.

TO DRY HERBS FOR WINTER USE

Gather herbs on a dry day. Spread on sheets of paper and dry quickly in sun, or near fire, or in cool oven with door open. Unless dried quickly, herbs lose their colour. Strip leaves from stalks and dry again if necessary, spreading them on baking sheets and finishing drying in oven. Leaves should be dried till they are crisp—this takes about 1 hour in oven. When dried, rub through a fine sieve, or crush with rolling pin to fine powder, put into hot bottles, cork tightly and store in dry place.

*   *   *   *   *

Any of the herbs mentioned herewith may be dried by this method. Use herbs fresh when in season and dry for winter.

The Thymes.—Used with discretion both lemon and common thyme are valuable aids to the cook in the flavouring of soups, stews and of forcemeats for veal, rabbit, poultry and pies. Dry in July and August.

Parsley.—Gives its name to popular English white sauce served with meat, fish and poultry, flavours vegetables and forcemeat and, finely chopped or in small sprigs, makes attractive garnish.

Mint.—Chiefly known in connection with the sauce that accompanies lamb and as flavouring for new potatoes, green peas and pea soup. Modern hostesses like it as garnish for long drinks and cups and the young green leaves are used in salad decoration.

Sage.—Flavours onion stuffing with pork and duck, also pork sausages. Is very good if used sparingly. A little goes a long way.

Tarragon.—An aromatic herb good with fish and, though dried and powdered like other herbs, is most convenient in the form of tarragon vinegar.

To make this vinegar put ¼ lb. tarragon leaves, stalked and bruised, into jam jar, cover with 1 pint vinegar. Cover jar to exclude air, leave 7 weeks in cool dry place. Strain through muslin; bottle.

Marjoram.—Several varieties of this herb, but sweet marjoram is the one preferred by the modern cook. Used in the same way as thyme and often with it in mixed herbal flavourings.

Sweet Herb Mixture.—A powder of mixed dried herbs ready at hand saves time in kitchen.

1 oz. thyme.	1½ ozs. parsley.
1 oz. lemon thyme.	1 oz. chervil.
1½ ozs. marjoram.	½ oz. tarragon.

Sift these herbs through sieve, taking care to see that no stalks remain. Preserve in closely corked bottle.

The Bouquet Garni.—Fragrant culinary posy, gathered fresh from the herb patch—a sprig of thyme, parsley and marjoram makes a simple bouquet which can be given more distinction when a bayleaf is added. Tie up in muslin and remove before serving any dish to which it has imparted its aromatic aid.

HOW TO USE THE SPICES

Ginger and cinnamon are two favourite spices today and both are used in the flavouring of sweet and savoury dishes and in cakes. Mace is much used in flavouring meats and sandwich pastes, savoury moulds and jellies. A grate of nutmeg improves many vegetables, including runner beans, and it is used sparingly or lavishly according to taste in puddings, cakes and sweet sauces. For a handy mixed spice to flavour savoury dishes allow :

1 oz. ground pepper.   ½ oz. powdered mace.
½ oz. powdered ginger.   ¼ oz. powdered cloves.

*   *   *   *   *

PART III

READERS' OWN TESTED RECIPES

USING the columns of their newspaper as Forum, women readers of *The Daily Telegraph* debate the special cookery problems of the seasons, eager to share with one another the knowledge special to home or district or gained by the light of experience. In this way the secrets of the farmhouse, the special dishes of the county town and the highly individualised cookery of the town flat become known to a far wider circle than would otherwise be possible.

These recipes are among those for which requests are being continually received, and are all recommended by readers.

CANDIED PEEL

Cut up orange peel, cover with cold water and 1 table-spoonful salt. Soak overnight, or longer if you want to collect peelings for a day or two. Drain, cover again with cold water, bring to boil, boil ½ hour, drain. Cover with hot water, boil until tender, about ¾ hour. Drain, measure, add ¾ cupful sugar to each cupful peel, return to saucepan with sugar and water and simmer until syrup is nearly gone. Store in jars, covering with syrup. This will keep well.

EGGLESS CHOCOLATE CAKE

8 dessertspoonfuls plain flour.	1 dessertspoonful baking powder.
3 dessertspoonfuls ground rice.	2 ozs. lard
6 dessertspoonfuls cocoa powder.	½ pint milk (sour milk or milk and water may be used).
7 dessertspoonfuls sugar.	

Mix all dry ingredients, rub in lard, add liquid to make the whole the consistency of a stiff batter. Bake in greaseproof paper-lined tin in moderate oven for about $1-1\frac{1}{2}$ hours, lowering oven heat a little after cake has risen.

GOLDEN SAUCE

Here is a sweet sauce which makes a simple pudding interesting, yet requires neither sugar, fat, flour, nor milk.

2 tablespoonfuls small sago.
2 tablespoonfuls golden syrup.
A few drops lemon flavouring.
One pint water.

Wash sago, put into water, and simmer till grains have practically disappeared. Add syrup, and lemon flavouring to taste. Simmer on very low heat till required—the longer it cooks the better. Serve hot with pudding.

GRILLED WELSH RAREBIT

4 ozs. cheese, grated.
¾ oz. margarine.
¼ teaspoonful mustard.
A little Worcester sauce or ketchup.
¾ dessertspoonful beer.

Cream all together well in a basin, adding a pinch of salt to taste. Spread mixture on toast. Place under grill to brown very slightly. Sufficient for 4 persons.

INCREASING BUTTER RATION

2 ozs. butter.
3 ozs. margarine.
1 gill milk.

Beat together butter and margarine in warmed basin. When creamed add milk, little by little. Beat for ½ hour, or until all milk is absorbed. Do not let butter and margarine become hot by overheating basin.

ANOTHER METHOD:—

¼ lb. butter.
¼ lb. margarine.
1 teaspoonful cornflour.
3 large tablespoonfuls milk.
Pinch of salt.

Add salt to cornflour, mix to a smooth paste with a little of the milk. Boil remainder of milk and stir into cornflour. Pour back into saucepan and cook a minute or two until it thickens, stirring all the time. Cool slightly. Cut up butter and margarine, beat together with a wooden spoon, stir in warm cornflour paste and beat till thoroughly mixed.

MANSFIELD FAIR PIES

This is an old Nottinghamshire recipe which requires green gooseberries, sugar and special pie pastry.

Make the crust with 6 oz. lard or lard and margarine and 1½ lb. flour, a pinch of salt, water to mix. Put fat into saucepan with water and bring to boil. Stir into flour and salt to make a very stiff dough. Roll out while hot and line some large deep patty pans or pie tins ; all sizes of Mansfield pies are made.

Pack as full as possible with gooseberries and add sugar to taste. Pour in a little water and put on a pastry lid. Make a small hole in centre, press edges together well and decorate top with fancy pastry cuttings. Bake in moderate oven from 1–1¼ hours, according to size. These are always eaten cold.

MOCK TONGUE

Ox heart.	2 tablespoonfuls sugar (brown preferably).
3 carrots.	
2 onions.	1 dessertspoonful powdered gelatine.
1 oz. pickling spice.	
1 piece root ginger.	Pepper.

Put heart in brine for a week, then wash well and put into a large pan together with the carrots and onions, pickling spice tied in a muslin bag, ginger, sugar and a little pepper. Cover with cold water and cook slowly three hours. Take 1 breakfast-cupful of liquid and dissolve the gelatine in it. Cut heart into neat slices, pack into a mould, pouring a little gelatine stock between each layer. Put rest of liquid on top and leave to set

Liquid and vegetables in which heart was cooked, put through a sieve, may be served as soup.

Now's the time to use
TOOTH POWDER

— the **IRIUM TOOTH POWDER** that **gives you a brighter smile, a fresher mouth!** If you've never used Pepsodent — the tooth powder with the PLUS ingredient, IRIUM, you simply have no idea how brilliant your teeth can look, how fresh-as-a-breeze your mouth can feel. IRIUM is the most powerful of all cleansing agents — yet the gentlest. It is so marvellously effective because IRIUM dissolves away every surface stain, every tiny treacherous particle. Now, more than ever, do you want to show a smiling face to the world. You will — if you use the IRIUM tooth powder. 7½d., 1/3 and 2/2 *including tax*

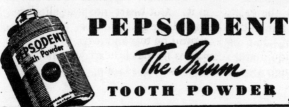

PEPSODENT
The Irium
TOOTH POWDER

PRUNE JAM

Wash the prunes, place in a preserving pan and just cover with cold water. Stew till tender and then put through a sieve.

Weigh the pulp and allow ½ lb. sugar to each pound. Melt the sugar in a pan with a little water, then add pulp. Boil for quarter of an hour, stirring frequently, then skim. Pour into jars and seal when cool.

SAVOURY CHEESE PUDDING

1½ cupfuls breadcrumbs.	1 egg.
¾–1 cupful grated cheese	Pepper and salt
1 cupful milk.	

Warm the milk in a saucepan, pour over breadcrumbs and cheese. Season well with pepper, but be sparing with salt. Let ingredients soak for a short time, then add the egg well beaten. Pour mixture into greased dish ; cook in moderate oven till set and delicately browned.

SAVOURY ROLY-POLY

½ lb. flour.	1 onion.
¼ lb. suet.	1 carrot.
1 teaspoonful baking powder.	Meat or vegetable stock or milk and water.
Left-overs of bacon, cold meat, or sausage.	Salt, pepper.

Mince left-overs, onion and carrot, add flour, baking powder, seasoning, shredded or chopped suet, and sufficient stock to make a soft dough. Shape into a roll. Tie in cloth and steam in usual way 2½ hours. Or mixture may be put into greased basin and steamed.

SOUR MILK DISHES

Cream Cheese.—Pour sour milk into thin cloth, tie up and leave to drip overnight, or until firm and all water has dripped off. Mix curd with a little margarine and sufficient milk to make thick puree. Add finely chopped onion or chives, season with salt and pepper.

Mock Welsh Rarebit.—Strain sour milk as above. Add a little made mustard, pepper and Worcester sauce to taste, and spread cheese on toast. Put under grill to brown.

Ciernikis (A Russian dish).

¼ lb. curd.	1 egg.
½ lb. flour.	Pinch of salt, pepper, nut
1 tablespoonful margarine.	meg.

Make a pastry of these ingredients and put in cool place for 1 hour. Roll out thinly and cut into rounds. Put into boiling salted water, boil in open saucepan 15–20 minutes. Strain and serve with brown melted margarine or tomato sauce.

SUGAR ECONOMY IN FRUIT COOKERY
(Three Methods)

(1) Rhubarb or gooseberries can be treated by this method. In the case of rhubarb cut into 1 inch pieces. Scald in saucepan with boiling water, leaving lid off. Bring to boil, remove at once from heat. Cover saucepan, leave 10 minutes, strain. Cook fruit as required, using less sugar.

(2) Cut up rhubarb, put in pan with good pinch of bicarbonate of soda, bring nearly to boil, pour off water, repeat process if very tart. Cook as usual.

(3) Prepare fruit the day before required. Sprinkle a little sugar on it. The following day sugar will have dissolved into syrup. Cook fruit slowly in syrup ; do not add any water.

TO CLARIFY DRIPPING

Boil together slowly dripping and cold water, removing scum as it rises. Cool slightly and pour into a basin. When set, remove cake of fat which will have settled on top of water. Scrape away sediment from the underside, return fat to saucepan, and heat gently until all water has evaporated. This ensures keeping.

TO CLARIFY FAT

Remove skin and gristle from fat, cut it into small pieces and bring to the boil in saucepan containing enough cold water to cover the pieces. Skim well, continue cooking slowly until water has evaporated and the liquid is clear and oily and pieces of fat look dried and sink to the bottom. Cool fat slightly, then strain through a cloth or fine wire strainer.

TO SERVE BEETROOTS HOT

Choose round, medium, even-sized beetroots. Wash carefully, leave on inch of stalk ; bake in moderately hot oven 1¼ hours. When done—test as for a baked potato— remove skins quickly. Pile beetroots on shallow dish, pour over a few drops of tarragon vinegar and salad oil.

Have ready a good white sauce, pour carefully round and through beets, but not over them, as the domes of bright red must show. Serve at once.

YORKSHIRE TRIPE ROLL

2 lbs. tripe.	One or two slices of brawn,
4 potatoes	or fat bacon or ham (op-
1 tablespoonful chopped parsley	tional).
	Nutmeg, flour, oil or fat.
1 tablespoonful chopped onions.	dripping.
	Seasoning.
2 cupfuls breadcrumbs	

Choose the tripe in one piece, suitable for rolling. Boil and mash potatoes. Add parsley, onions, breadcrumbs, ham, bacon or brawn, chopped finely, seasoning and a touch of nutmeg. If too dry add enough milk to bind. Lay tripe on a board and spread with mixture. Roll tightly and tie with string. Roll in flour, then in oil or melted fat, and again in flour. Place in baking tin with dripping, and bake 1 hour in hot oven. Cut in slices for serving and cover with hot tomato sauce.

PART IV

CANTEEN COOKERY ADAPTED TO HOME KITCHEN

WOMEN whose only training has been their own kitchen are running communal kitchens and canteens successfully. From the daily routine of providing for a household of three or four people, they have undertaken the strenuous, expert job of caring for ten or even a hundred times that number.

Today they work under local and other authorities instead of in the country-house soup kitchen of a century ago. Buying in quantity has become a highly responsible business, requiring experience and knowledge of the trades concerned. Cooking in large quantities differs from domestic cookery.

Take for instance the communal hotpot. The vegetables seem to "season" the meat and very little more seasoning is required than for the small family dish.

While the home background of communal cookery has gone, the dishes change little. Recipes given here are for old favourites which are constantly served today.

Quantities are for 20 people, this being a useful figure which can be reduced for family catering or multiplied for the canteen that serves many people.

MOCK TURTLE SOUP

Few bones (calf's head if obtainable).	Bacon rinds.
6 lbs. mixed vegetables— all kinds in season, including potato.	1 dessertspoonful mixed herbs.
	Gravy browning, water.

Place cut-up vegetables with bones and bacon rinds in stewpan. Well cover with water and let simmer for 2 hours. Now add herbs and browning, season to taste and bring to boil. Strain and serve.

EGGLESS TOAD-IN-THE-HOLE

6 lbs. sausages.	1 quart milk and water (half each).
4 lbs. flour.	
1 dessertspoonful baking powder.	1 tablespoonful egg substitute.
1 teaspoonful salt.	½ teacupful warm water
	Dripping.

Beat up egg substitute well in water, let it stand all night. Sieve flour, salt and baking powder into basin, make well in centre. Pour in egg substitute, stir in flour, adding milk and water gradually to make batter. Beat well. Cover and leave at least 2 hours. Melt fat in baking tin, when really hot pour in batter, group sausages in pairs in batter (this simplifies the serving of portions). Bake in hot oven.

LIVER AND SAUSAGE PIE

3 lbs. liver.	3 lbs. mixed vegetables.
2 lbs. sausages.	Gravy, seasoning.
	Pastry.

Slice liver, skin and slice sausages, dice vegetables, place all in stewpan, well cover with water. Simmer ½ hour. Thicken and colour with gravy, adding seasoning to taste ; sausages sometimes make it salt enough.

Turn into pie dishes and cover with pastry as for steak and kidney pie.

STEAK, KIDNEY AND VEGETABLE PIE

2 lbs. steak and kidney.	½ teaspoonful salt.
4 lbs. mixed vegetables— carrots, turnips, onions, parsnips, celery.	2 tablespoonfuls flour.
	1 teacupful water.
½ teaspoonful pepper.	Gravy browning.

For Pastry

¼ lb. mashed potato.	2 lbs. self-raising flour.
½ lb. cooking fat or margarine.	1 teaspoonful salt.
	Water.

Meat and vegetables should be diced ½ inch square;

stew until tender. Thicken with flour and water made into a paste. Add a little gravy browning and season.

To make pastry, rub fat into flour, add mashed potato (warmed, as it will mix in better) and salt. Make into a smooth dough with water. Roll out, cover pie in usual way, bake in a good oven.

Any pastry left can be made into patties which provide snacks for supper.

VEAL, HAM AND VEGETABLE PIE

This is a good way of using the very fat bacon from overseas.

2 lbs. pie veal.	½ teaspoonful salt.
2 lbs. bacon.	½ teaspoonful pepper.
3 lbs. vegetables.	

The method is the same as for steak, kidney and vegetable pie.

MUTTON AND SAUSAGE HOT-POT

You can be more generous with meat in this dish, as the cuts are cheaper than for steak and kidney pie.

3 lbs. breast and scrag of mutton.	2 lbs. potatoes.
	Salt, pepper.
2 lbs. sausages.	Stock or water.
4 lbs. mixed vegetables.	

Cut breast and scrag as for Irish stew, skin and slice sausages and vegetables, including potatoes. Into a deep baking tin place layer of meat and sausage, then vegetables, but not potatoes, continue with layers, and season them. Well cover meat and vegetables with stock or water. Lastly, lay on the sliced potatoes. Place in oven and let it cook gently for about 1 hour.

APPLE CONDE

This sweet is served cold in sundae glasses.

5 lbs. apples.	3 lbs. rice.
½ lb. sugar or syrup to sweeten.	2 tablespoonfuls cornflour or potato flour.
Pinch of salt to bring out sweetness.	Milk, water.

Peel apples, cover and cut into four. Place in shallow pan or dish with sugar. Cover with water and cook very gently to keep pieces intact. When cooked take apple out of syrup and boil syrup up again. Add cornflour or potato flour made into a paste with water or milk. Cook rice with as little water as possible, then stir in a little milk. To serve, make heaps of rice in sundae glasses, build apples on top and coat with syrup. Appearance is improved if syrup is coloured with a drop or two of cochineal.

DELHI ROLL

6 lbs. self-raising flour.	1½ lbs. mashed potato
1¼ lbs. fat or suet.	3 pints water.

For Filling

3 lbs. cut-up apples.	¼ lb. cut-up dates or figs.
½ lb. currants.	1 teaspoonful spice.

Rub fat or stir suet into flour, add potato, warmed, make into a rather stiff dough with water. Let it stand 10–15 minutes, roll out, sprinkle the filling mixture over it, roll up like a jam roll. Steam 1½ hours, and serve with custard sauce.

INDIVIDUAL GOLDEN SPONGE PUDDINGS

8 lbs. self-raising flour.	Milk and water to make 2 quarts.
1¼ lbs. cooking fat.	
1½ lbs. mashed potato.	Syrup or jam.

Rub fat into flour, add mashed potato, warmed. Make a loose dough with milk and water. Grease small pudding moulds, put a little syrup or jam at bottom and three parts fill with the mixture; steam 1 hour.

As an alternative to jam or syrup, serve with custard sauce.

FIREFIGHTERS' CAKES

These were served to firefighters after having been made for them in a sixth-floor City kitchen during the height of a blitz.

8 lbs. self-raising flour.	2 tablespoonfuls baking powder.
1½ lbs. cooking fat or margarine.	1 lb. sugar.
1½ lbs. mashed potato.	Milk and water to make 2 quarts (or water only will do).
1 lb. currants and 1 lb. sultanas or 2 lbs. chopped dates.	

Rub fat into flour and baking powder sieved together, add other ingredients, including mashed potato, warmed. Make to a stiff dough with milk and water as quickly as possible. Put mixture in small heaps on baking sheet; bake in hot oven 30 minutes.

To make rice cakes, leave out fruit, and make dough into little balls. Paint the tops with flour and water paste, take each up and dip in castor sugar or ground rice.

WARTIME ECLAIRS

This recipe makes 40 eclair cases with filling of vanilla cream.

¼ lb. margarine.	¼ lb. flour.
¼ pint water.	2 eggs.

Put margarine and water in saucepan, bring to boil. Add flour and stir. Place back on stove until mixture is dry and leaves pan. Remove from heat, add eggs, one at a time, while mixture is still hot, and beat in

thoroughly. Make paper cornet to use as forcing bag.
Fill with mixture which should be pressed out into
eclair, shell or any other shape desired.

Bake in medium oven 350°F. till golden brown.
Watch for this colour, if paler they will go flat.

Vanilla Cream Filling

For filling, make an ordinary vanilla custard with 2 ozs·
custard powder and ½ pint milk. Add 2 tablespoonfuls
powdered gelatine or 1½ ozs. leaf gelatine while custard is
still warm. Beat 5 minutes. Let it set, then fill cases.
Dash with jam.

INDEX